YORK NOTES

EDUCATING RITA

WILLY RUSSELL

NOTES BY TONY RAWDIN

 Longman

 York Press

The right of Tony Rawdin to be identified as Author of this Work
has been asserted by him in accordance with the
Copyright, Designs and Patents Act 1988

YORK PRESS
322 Old Brompton Road, London SW5 9JH

PEARSON EDUCATION LIMITED
Edinburgh Gate, Harlow,
Essex CM20 2JE, United Kingdom
Associated companies, branches and representatives throughout the world

First published 1998
This new and fully revised edition first published 2003
Third impression 2003

10 9 8 7 6 5 4 3

ISBN 0-582-77266-4

Designed by Michelle Cannatella
Illustrated by Susan Scott
Typeset by Land & Unwin (Data Sciences), Bugbrooke, Northamptonshire
Produced by Pearson Education Asia Limited, Hong Kong

CONTENTS

PART ONE
INTRODUCTION

How to study a play 5
Author and context 6
Setting and background 7
Timeline 10

PART TWO
SUMMARIES

General summary 14
Detailed summaries
Act I, Scenes 1–4...16
Act I, Scenes 5–8 27
Act II, Scenes 1–3 36
Act II, Scenes 4–7 43

PART THREE
COMMENTARY

Themes...51
Structure 54
Characters 55
Language and style 59

PART FOUR
RESOURCES

How to use quotations 63
Coursework essay...64
Sitting the examination 65
Improve your grade...66
Sample essay plan 73
Further questions 74

LITERARY TERMS 76

CHECKPOINT HINTS/ANSWERS 77

TEST ANSWERS 80

PREFACE

York Notes are designed to give you a broader perspective on works of literature studied at GCSE and equivalent levels. With examination requirements changing in the twenty-first century, we have made a number of significant changes to this new series. We continue to help students to reach their own interpretations of the text but York Notes now have important extra-value new features.

You will discover that York Notes are genuinely interactive. The new **Checkpoint** features make sure that you can test your knowledge and broaden your understanding. You will also be directed to excellent websites, books and films where you can follow up ideas for yourself.

The **Resources** section has been updated and an entirely new section has been devoted to how to improve your grade. Careful reading and application of the principles laid out in the Resources section guarantee improved performance.

The **Detailed summaries** include an easy-to-follow skeleton structure of the story-line, while the section on **Language and style** has been extended to offer an in-depth discussion of the writer's techniques.

The Contents page shows the structure of this study guide. However, there is no need to read from the beginning to the end as you would with a novel, play or poem. Use the Notes in the way that suits you. Our aim is to help you with your understanding of the work, not to dictate how you should learn.

Our authors are practising English teachers and examiners who have used their experience to offer a whole range of **Examiner's secrets** – useful hints to encourage exam success.

The General Editor of this series is John Polley, Senior GCSE Examiner and former Head of English at Harrow Way Community School, Andover.

The author of these Notes, Tony Rawdin, has worked as a Head of English in two comprehensive schools in the north of England, and acted as a Senior Examiner for a large Examination Board for a number of years. He is currently a Deputy Head teacher in North Yorkshire.

The text used in these Notes is the Longman edition, 1991.

PART ONE

INTRODUCTION

HOW TO STUDY A PLAY

Though it may seem obvious, remember that a play is written to be performed before an audience. Ideally, you should see the play live on stage. A film or video recording is next best, though neither can capture the enjoyment of being in a theatre and realising that your reactions are part of the performance.

There are six aspects of a play:

❶ THE PLOT: a play is a story whose events are carefully organised by the playwright in order to show how a situation can be worked out

❷ THE CHARACTERS: these are the people who have to face this situation. Since they are human they can be good or bad, clever or stupid, likeable or detestable, etc. They may change too!

❸ THE THEMES: these are the underlying messages of the play, e.g. jealousy can cause the worst of crimes; ambition can bring the mightiest low

❹ THE SETTING: this concerns the time and place that the author has chosen for the play

❺ THE LANGUAGE: the writer uses a certain style of expression to convey the characters and ideas

❻ STAGING AND PERFORMANCE: the type of stage, the lighting, the sound effects, the costumes, the acting styles and delivery must all be decided

Work out the choices the dramatist has made in the first four areas, and consider how a director might balance these choices to create a live performance.

The purpose of these York Notes is to help you understand what the play is about and to enable you to make your own interpretation. Do not expect the study of a play to be neat and easy: plays are chosen for examination purposes, not written for them!

DID YOU KNOW?
Educating Rita won the 1980 Society of West End Theatres award for best comedy.

AUTHOR – LIFE AND WORKS

1947 Born in Whiston, Liverpool

1962 Left school, eventually working as a ladies' hairdresser

1970 Trained as a teacher

1972 St Catherine's College Drama Group perform Willy Russell's *Keep Your Eyes Down* at the Edinburgh Fringe Festival

1973 Commissioned by Everyman Theatre in Liverpool *King of the Castle* (TV)

1974 *John, Paul, George, Ringo and...Bert Break In (TV)*; *Death of a Young Man (TV)*

1975 *Breezeblock Park*

1977 *Our Day Out* (TV)

1978 *Stags and Hens* (Filmed as *Dancing through the dark*)

1979 *Boy with the transistor radio* (TV) *The Daughters of Albion* (TV)

1980 *Educating Rita* – play wins West End Best Comedy Award

1983 *Educating Rita* released on film, Willy Russell awarded Honorary MA by Open University for his work as a playwright
Blood Brothers
Our Day Out
One Summer (TV)

1986 *Shirley Valentine*

1993 *Terraces* (TV)

CONTEXT

1948 Introduction of the National Health Service

1950s Rock n' roll sweeps Britain from America

1952 Death of George VI

1953 Coronation of Queen Elizabeth II

1957 Prime Minister Harold Macmillan declares 'most of our people have never had it so good'

1960s Wide social change and the beginnings of the 'permissive society'

1963 *Please please me* becomes the Beatles' first no.1 hit and Beatlemania grips the nation

1965 Death Penalty abolished

1966 England win the World Cup

1967 Abortion Act legalises the termination of pregnancies

1969 Neil Armstrong is first man on the moon; Divorce Reform Act

1970s Education reform and the introduction of comprehensive schools

1970 Germaine Greer publishes her book *The Female Eunuch*, inspiring the women's liberation movement

1973 Britain becomes a member of the European Union

1975 Equal Opportunities Act

1979 Margaret Thatcher becomes first female Prime Minister

SETTING AND BACKGROUND

Willy Russell was born in 1947 in Whiston, just outside Liverpool. His father was a factory worker, until he gave it up to buy a fish and chip shop. His mother had a menial job in a warehouse. The young Russell, therefore, had the sort of upbringing which failed to indicate any sort of literary potential, let alone suggest a career of writing which would establish himself as one of the most popular and successful **playwrights** of modern times.

DID YOU KNOW?

Willy Russell still lives in Liverpool, the city of his birth.

EDUCATION

At school, by his own admission, Willy Russell failed to excel. He did enjoy reading though, and it was during this period of his life that he first dreamed of becoming a writer. However, believing this to be a foolish notion for someone of his class, he buried the thought deep within himself for many years. Rather like Rita in *Educating Rita*, it was only in adulthood that he could break away from the pressure of his peers and follow his own desire for education.

EARLY EMPLOYMENT

After failing his Apprentice Printer's examination, Russell acted on his mother's suggestion and became a qualified ladies' hairdresser, eventually running his own small salon. He never really enjoyed this job and claims that he was never any good at it either, but on quiet days it did at least provide him with the opportunity to begin writing. This led to him passing 'O' Level English Literature at night school and a short spell working at a car factory earned him enough money to enrol full time at college. It is easy to see that there are definite parallels between his own life and the experiences of his fictional character, Rita.

CHECKPOINT 1

What parallels can you see between Willy Russell and the character of Rita?

OTHER WORKS

Apart from *Educating Rita*, which was written in 1979, Willy Russell has written a number of other popular and successful plays such as *Breezeblock Park* (1975), *One for the Road* (1976), *Our Day Out* (1977), *Stags and Hens* (1978) and *Blood Brothers* (1981). Perhaps his most celebrated work, other than *Educating Rita*, is the play *Shirley Valentine* (1986). Both have been adapted for the cinema and turned into highly acclaimed films.

The opening of *Educating Rita* states that the events are set in a university somewhere '*in the north of England*' (p. 1). However, there can be little doubt that Rita's broad Scouse accent locates the play more specifically in Liverpool, Willy Russell's home town. Despite this, the play has a distinctly universal appeal. Rita reflects, at first glance, a working-class desire to escape from her own culture and background, in order to lead an apparently more fulfilling life in the type of society represented by Frank and the other students with whom she comes into contact.

THE WORKING CLASS BACKGROUND

Rita claims that the working class has effectively lost its culture and all she sees are people who are 'pissed, or on the Valium, tryin' to get from one day to the next' (p. 30).

There appears to be no meaning to their lives. When Rita fails to find the necessary self-confidence to attend Frank's dinner party one Saturday night, she meets up with the rest of her family in the local pub instead. Although everyone appears to be happy as they all sing together, Rita senses that this is simply a thin veneer and the tears shed by her mother would appear to justify this. Clearly, Rita's

DID YOU KNOW?
The 1970s were times of great social change and, since the play was written, people have been forced to think again about what constitutes being 'working class'.

mother thinks there ought to be more to life than the humdrum existence they are leading.

Although society has altered radically since then, *Educating Rita* is now more relevant than ever. The more divided that society becomes, the greater the need for the impoverished people to escape. Moreover, the play can be viewed on a purely personal level. Here is a woman whose lack of fulfilment must be shared by many people who sit in the audience and witness Rita's attempts to change herself and her situation. She experiences problems in her marriage, and her husband's desire for her to have children only throws the dilemma into sharper focus. How can Rita have children when she knows that she is not ready for the responsibility? She yearns for something substantial in her life and realises that she must 'discover meself first' (p. 12).

The play is **naturalistic** in the sense that all the action takes place in Frank's study. By doing so, Willy Russell is taking Rita out of her world and immersing her in Frank's. The room itself is significant. The fact that it is set in a Victorian-built university suggests tradition and permanence. The rows and rows of books which dominate the stage represent the world of knowledge to which Rita aspires and they enable her to experience life in a variety of forms. Although her experiences are second-hand, they do allow Rita to change into an entirely different person.

ACADEMIC BACKGROUND

Frank's cultural background is entirely alien to Rita when she first attends the Open University course, but she is determined to fit in with his social and academic circles. In doing so, she proposes to alter her whole way of living. Instead of spending evenings in the pub, she chooses to visit the theatre. Her choice of books, clothes and even her job is governed by a burning desire to be accepted into Frank's world, all of which seems **ironic** in view of the fact that Frank himself is certainly not happy with his own lifestyle. Divorced and now struggling to maintain a relationship with Julia, one of his ex-students, his dissatisfaction with life is reflected in his inability to write the sort of poetry he would like and a growing drink problem.

CHECKPOINT 2

What examples are there to show that Denny, Rita's husband, does not share Rita's desire to change?

 DID YOU KNOW?

Although the setting is described as a '*university in the north of England*', most directors have chosen to base the events more specifically in Liverpool.

CHECKPOINT 3

What examples can you find to show that Rita struggles to fit into Frank's world?

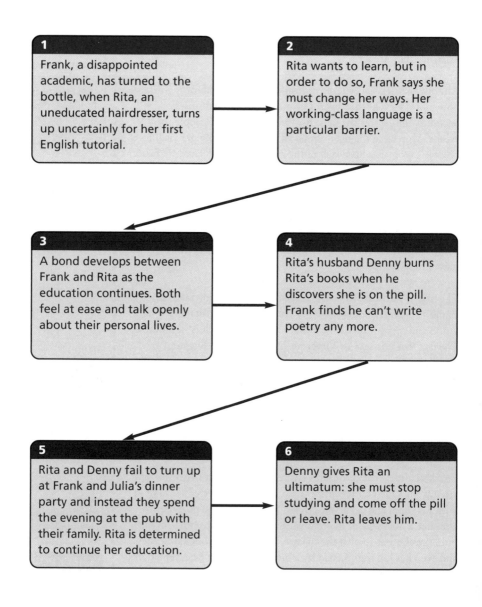

1
Frank, a disappointed academic, has turned to the bottle, when Rita, an uneducated hairdresser, turns up uncertainly for her first English tutorial.

2
Rita wants to learn, but in order to do so, Frank says she must change her ways. Her working-class language is a particular barrier.

3
A bond develops between Frank and Rita as the education continues. Both feel at ease and talk openly about their personal lives.

4
Rita's husband Denny burns Rita's books when he discovers she is on the pill. Frank finds he can't write poetry any more.

5
Rita and Denny fail to turn up at Frank and Julia's dinner party and instead they spend the evening at the pub with their family. Rita is determined to continue her education.

6
Denny gives Rita an ultimatum: she must stop studying and come off the pill or leave. Rita leaves him.

7

Summer school is a turning point for Rita. She finds a flatmate Trish and becomes a 'proper' student. She is more self-confident too.

8

Frank's drinking gets him into trouble with the university authorities when he falls off the stage while giving a lecture.

9

Frank becomes fearful of losing Rita to her new friends. His drinking becomes worse. He gives Rita his poetry and asks her to write an essay on it.

10

Rita values Frank's poetry but Frank feels increasingly worthless. Their relationship begins to break down. Rita sits her examination.

11

Frank, now partnerless, prepares to leave for Australia and a fresh start. He recognises Rita has lost her uniqueness.

12

An independent, self-assured Rita passes her exams and Frank gives her a present of a dress. Rita cuts his long hair.

Act I

Act II

PART TWO

SUMMARIES

GENERAL SUMMARY

The play is about Rita's attempt to break free from her mundane existence as a hairdresser and enter fully and with confidence into Frank's academic, middle-class world.

ACT I

Dissatisfied with his academic career, Frank has turned to the bottle to forget his pain, and even before Rita arrives for her tutorial he has already contemplated a visit to the pub to 'wash away the memory of some silly woman's attempt to get into the mind of Henry James' (p. 2).

Rita's first, clumsy entry reflects her social inferiority. Ill at ease and finding it difficult to break into Frank's world, her strong Liverpudlian accent clearly identifies her as coming from a completely different background.

To Frank, Rita is like 'the first breath of air' (p. 11) that has been in his room for years, but he feels uneasy in his role as a tutor for the Open University and attempts to persuade Rita to change tutors. However, a bond rapidly emerges between the two characters and Rita is adamant that Frank will educate her, because he is 'a crazy mad piss artist who wants to throw his students through the window' (p. 14).

In trying to escape from one world and enter into another, Rita finds that many conflicts emerge. Her husband's lack of support means that she has to write her essays in quiet moments at work (hardly ideal conditions for study!). This conflict deepens when Denny burns her books, on finding out that Rita had been taking the contraceptive pill against his wishes. The relationship cannot sustain such conflict and, eventually, the marriage breaks down.

CHECKPOINT 4

What examples can you find to illustrate Rita's and Frank's differing use of language?

CHECKPOINT 5

Rita's marriage breaks down as a result of her education, but what would have happened if Denny had supported her?

The first half of the play ends with Rita coming to a crossroads in her development. She could turn the clock back and return to her former way of life, but decides against this. Instead, she determines to press on with her education and, with renewed vigour, to channel all her energy into the learning process.

ACT II

As Act II gets under way, we immediately detect a change in the relationship between Frank and Rita. Following her success at summer school, she is brimming with confidence and she has found another sort of teacher in Trish, her new flatmate: 'She's dead classy. Y' know like, she's got taste, y' know like you, Frank, she's just got it' (p. 51).

We now become more aware of Frank's own weaknesses. His drinking is taking such a hold upon his life that Rita is forced to warn him that 'It'll kill y', Frank' (p. 54). His marriage has already broken down and his relationship with Julia seems to be under threat. At the centre of all this is Frank's inability to write the sort of poetry that he would like. A sense of failure and frustration spills over into his teaching and, possibly to escape the consequences, he turns to the whisky bottle for comfort. As Rita searches for her true self, it seems that Frank is losing his own sense of identity.

In the later scenes of the play, we witness their relationship breaking down. The conflict between Rita and Denny in Act I gives way to a conflict between Rita and Frank in Act II and Frank is scathing about Rita's lack of real learning. He tries to make amends by calling her about the examination and, in the final scene, Rita comes to thank Frank for being a good teacher. Having passed her examination, she can now choose her own direction in life. Frank, meanwhile, asks her to accompany him to Australia, following his banishment by the university authorities.

The play ends on a lighter note with Rita preparing to give Frank a haircut. The audience is aware of the sexual undertones when Rita tells Frank 'I never thought there was anythin' I could give you. But there is. Come here, Frank ...', but Willy Russell undercuts this with the final line, 'I'm gonna take ten years off you ...' (p. 73).

 DID YOU KNOW?

From the earliest times, there has been a link between drinking alcohol and writing. Even in Greek mythology, Bacchus or Dionysus was worshipped as the God of wine and was believed to inspire poetry.

CHECKPOINT 6

How does Frank make matters worse between himself and Rita?

Detailed Summaries

Scene 1 – Rita begins her 'education' with Frank

❶ Rita makes a clumsy first entrance.

❷ Frank attempts to persuade Rita to find a different tutor.

❸ The audience is made aware of Frank's drink problem.

? DID YOU KNOW?

All the 'action' of the play takes place in Frank's study. Other important 'scenes' of the play that take place outside this room are reported by Frank or Rita.

The opening scene, as for the entire play, is set in a first-floor room of a Victorian-built university in the north of England.

When the curtain rises, we see Frank, who is in his early fifties, busily searching along rows of bookshelves to find a hidden bottle of whisky. Now a rather disenchanted English lecturer, he has no enthusiasm for the Open University course on which Rita has enrolled. Note the **stage directions** which describe the scene. Be aware of these as you are reading the play.

CHECKPOINT 7

Can you find other examples of how Russell uses an entrance for comic effect?

The first scene opens up Rita's character, enabling the audience to see why she has been driven to join the course. Rita's first entry is a clumsy affair, rattling at the door knob and unable to get in. However, there is an air of determination about her which Frank finds impossible to ignore. She is like a 'breath of air' (p. 11), different from all the other students, and it is this freshness which is so appealing.

When talking about the picture of a nude religious scene hanging on Frank's wall, Rita asks her tutor whether or not he thinks of it as erotic. On hearing Frank's reply, 'I suppose it is', Rita's reaction is to state, 'There's no suppose about it. Look at those tits' (p. 3). This is typical of Rita and Frank's conversation as they get acquainted.

> **CHECKPOINT 8**
>
> How does Russell bring out humour in the play?

Their subjects of conversation quickly change, Rita offering Frank a cigarette and talking about people being afraid of death, which then reminds her of a poem on the same topic. Frank immediately assumes that Rita is speaking of the celebrated Welsh poet, Dylan Thomas, only to be told that she is, in fact referring to a poem by the contemporary Liverpool writer, Roger McGough. Not surprisingly, Frank has to admit, 'I don't think I know the actual piece you mean ...' (p. 5).

We learn that Rita's real name is Susan and that she is calling herself by this new name after Rita Mae Brown, the authoress of her favourite novel entitled *Rubyfruit Jungle*. Frank is clearly not impressed by such writing.

They then talk about E.M. Forster, the educated class life in comparison to Rita's, Yeats and Rita's learning. Rita talks about life at the hairdressers, herself and how at twenty-six, she feels 'out of step' (p. 12); while everyone else is expecting her to settle down and have children in the near future, Rita wants to discover herself first. Rita is attempting to create a new identity for herself. She is searching for a new meaning in her life and Frank is that means to an end. This lack of education but clear desire to learn is revealed in many ways in this scene, for instance when Rita asks Frank what **assonance** means. Education is a way for Rita to escape from her working-class surroundings.

CHECK THE NET

www.learn.co.uk
This site has lots of useful material to help you with your understanding and appreciation of the play.

Partly fearful of taking on such a burdensome responsibility and partly because of the course's unsocial hours that limit his drinking time, Frank encourages Rita to change tutors. Initially, she exits only to return moments later with the command, 'you are my teacher – an' you're gonna bleedin' well teach me' (p. 14). And if Frank was left in any doubt as to what he was taking on with his new student, he could not fail to realise it when Rita closes the scene with her assertion that she will cut his hair at the next meeting.

CHECKPOINT 9

What are the reasons that Rita seems so out of place?

At this stage of Rita's development, we see that she is desperate to find herself but does not know where to begin. She obviously feels that the change of name is important and yet casual observers would recognise that this is entirely superficial.

It is the mismatch between Rita's language and the academic **setting** that is the source of much humour in the play. Her accent and **dialect** clearly set her apart and so too does the constant swearing and joking. However, sometimes it is her lack of knowledge that marks the difference: 'Do you know Yeats?' says Frank. 'The wine lodge?' comes the reply (p. 8).

It is interesting to note that since the play was written, Roger McGough has continued to receive wide critical acclaim. Frank is dismissive of this poet and, **ironically**, it takes Rita to indicate his true ability. Significantly, by the end of the play, the audience has become all too aware that Frank is having problems writing his own poetry and that he would give anything to be able to write as freely as McGough.

CHECKPOINT 10

Why does Frank change his mind and agree to act as Rita's tutor?

Frank's own lack of confidence is highlighted in his attempt to persuade Rita to find another tutor. Although he maintains that the reason for this is because the evening course interferes with his drinking, one suspects that Frank is frightened of the challenge which faces him. Unlike most of his other students who could, by and large, get along without him, Rita is totally reliant on Frank for her education.

Rita is already beginning to find her feet to some extent. At the end of the scene Rita calls Frank a 'geriatric hippie' (p. 14), reflecting the confidence and security she feels in his company. Although it takes much longer for her to mix effectively with his regular students, the fact that Rita strikes up an immediate rapport with Frank is significant if she is to develop.

SCENE 2 – Rita's first tutorial

1 Frank struggles to get Rita to focus on E.M. Forster.
2 The audience learns of Rita's previous education.
3 Frank reveals details of his broken relationships.

Rita's second entrance involves Frank, along with the audience, witnessing the door handle being turned and turned again, but no one entering. When Frank finally opens the door, he reveals Rita, oil can in hand, trying to fix the faulty handle. She announces that she is doing it because she knows he will not.

Education and life

In this scene, the audience are made aware of the fact that both Frank and Rita are seen as 'incomplete' beings. Rita craves an education that will provide her with the opportunities to choose her own destiny. By following the crowd at school and underachieving, Rita now feels frustrated and unfulfilled. Although she is married and has a job as a hairdresser, she yearns for something greater.

By way of contrast, Frank has had an excellent education and yet he, too, has failed to achieve a sense of fulfilment. Not only is the audience allowed to see a number of failed relationships, but we also witness his bouts of heavy drinking and his declining powers of poetic creativity, all three of which may be inextricably linked. Willy Russell seems to be suggesting that, although education in itself does not guarantee happiness and personal fulfilment, it does provide individuals like Rita with the power to make choices.

GLOSSARY
geriatric hippie The hippies of the 1960s rejected traditional values and grew their hair long. Frank's hairstyl;e makes him look like an ageing hippie.

CHECK THE FILM

Willy Russell's interest in the portrayal of women was extended after this play to include an analysis of another Liverpudlian character, Shirley Valentine.

Once inside, Rita walks round Frank's room looking at various objects, admiring her tutor's taste, and trying to familiarise herself with her new surroundings. When she looks out of the window at the lawns, she asks Frank whether the 'proper' students sit down there to study, clearly distinguishing herself as not a 'proper' student. This shows her lack of confidence in her new environment, and also has much to do with her simply not understanding the realities of university education. As with her change of name, we recognise that in searching for her identity, she is simply moving further away from her true self. Her use of language is a barrier, the strong **accent** and **dialect** clearly pitching her in the working class and setting her apart from the rest of the students. This, in turn, leads to a certain lack of confidence on Rita's part; something which she is only able to overcome in the second half of the play. Rita describes how, as a child, she had a yearning to attend boarding school because of her vision of 'tuck-shop', 'matron' and 'prep' (p. 16). She describes her dissatisfaction with her own schooling: 'borin', ripped-up books, broken glass everywhere, knives an' fights.' Although she jokes, 'An' that was just the staffroom' (p. 17) the audience senses that there is a serious issue underlying all this cheerful banter. Rita explains that although the teachers tried their best, she was unable to commit herself to her education because there was no academic atmosphere. Studying was for the 'whimps' (p. 17), as she puts it, and for her to take school seriously she would have had to become different from her friends.

CHECKPOINT 11

What are the problems faced by Rita in restarting her education?

She now considers that it was this need for conformity that led to a rather shallow existence: music, clothes and 'lookin' for a feller' (p. 17) seemed to be the sum total of her experience. Rita comments that buying a new dress to change the external appearance can deflect you from the need to change yourself on the inside. Now, as a **symbolic** gesture, Rita is wearing an old dress and is refusing to buy another until she passes her first exam. By then, she hopes to have become an entirely new person and will be able to buy the 'sort of dress you'd only see on an educated woman' (p. 18).

The tutorial itself revolves around the E.M. Forster novel *Howards End*, which Rita had taken to read on her first visit. As with her appreciation of *Rubyfruit Jungle*, Rita responds to the text in a purely subjective manner, and it is Frank's task to develop in Rita a sense of critical detachment that will enable her to pass the examination.

Frank talks of Rita disciplining her mind and we see how she is unable to concentrate on the real business of the tutorial, choosing to probe into Frank's personal life instead. Here, we learn of Frank's marriage break-up and his new life with Julia, his early volumes of poetry and his recent inability to write.

Both characters open their souls and there is tension in the line, 'Rita – why didn't you walk in here twenty years ago?' (p. 23), but Rita extricates herself from an uncomfortable situation with the humorous retort, 'Cos I don't think they would have accepted me at the age of six' (p. 23). There is clearly a strong attraction and closeness between Frank and Rita, but Rita always does her best to play it down. The scene ends with Frank trying once again to focus Rita's attention on the Forster novel.

Willy Russell begins to develop the **theme** of education through Rita's story of her schooldays, and the idea is picked up later when she relates how she once saw a beautiful bird as a child but refrained from telling the teacher because she knew that the teacher would 'make us write an essay on it' (p. 22). Frank acknowledges this, and the **analogy** with the bird is related to Rita's own situation. He knows that for Rita to pass an examination in English Literature she

CHECK THE BOOK

Howards End, by E.M. Forster. Forster was born in London in 1879 and, after the death of his father, was brought up by his mother and great Aunt at Rooksnest, a house that inspired the country estate in *Howards End*.

CHECKPOINT 12

What other examples can you find to show Frank's physical attraction towards Rita?

CHECKPOINT 13

As *Educating Rita* develops, how does it become apparent that *both* characters are learning from each other?

must do more than simply admire the beauty of great works; she must also analyse them and communicate her ideas in writing.

Willy Russell's use of humour becomes more pronounced in this scene as the two characters begin to feed off each other. Rita's rather coarse and vulgar humour is countered by Frank's dry wit and the two contrasting styles work well together.

SCENE 3 – Frank has his work cut out!

❶ Rita's first essay shows how much Rita is lacking in terms of a formal education.

❷ Frank persuades Rita that she must develop her taste in literature.

 DID YOU KNOW?
Attitudes towards education have changed, partly as a result of works like *Educating Rita* which promote a return to learning. The concept of 'lifelong learning' is now more well established in society.

Rita is struggling to come to terms with E.M. Forster's novel *Howards End*. She pronounces, 'This Forster, honest to God he doesn't half get on my tits' (p. 24) to which Frank replies, 'Good. You must show me the evidence' (p. 24). This quick-witted reply reflects the closeness that is developing in their relationship.

When Frank asks Rita to compare *Howards End* to two other novels she has read that week, her reply depicts the difficulties she is finding in the traditional learning process.

Rita's essay on Forster refers almost entirely to the popular novelist Harold Robbins, and Frank is unimpressed. He stresses the need for her to develop taste in literature for, if she fails to appreciate anything other than pulp fiction, she will never be prepared for the examination. The final part of the scene suggests that Rita is finally getting the message when she admits 'My mind's full of junk' and 'It needs a good clearin' out' (p. 26).

Willy Russell said that this scene could be omitted when performing the play because it is not strictly essential in terms of the development of the **plot**. It is worth considering, however, what the play would lose by its omission.

Frank's attitude towards Rita and her education, after his early indifference, is very positive. A bond is emerging between the two characters and their relationship benefits them both. Rita receives the education which she craves and Frank, for his part, is given a new lease of life by Rita's exuberant enthusiasm.

When Rita confesses that the past week has been 'dead quiet in the shop' (p. 25) so she has been able to read three novels, it prepares us for her later admission that she writes her essays there too. This is the first indication that all is not well with her marriage to Denny and, more particularly, that he is not supporting her in her studies.

CHECKPOINT 14

What evidence is there to suggest that Rita's marriage is destined to fail?

In trying to understand Frank's comment that she can continue to read her racy novels as long as she doesn't write about them in the examination, Rita has to put the concept into her own language before she fully grasps his meaning: 'You mean, it's all right to go out an' have a bit of slap an' tickle with the lads as long as you don't go home an' tell your mum?' (p. 26). Throughout the rest of the play, Rita's intellectual development goes hand-in-hand with the development of her language.

The openings and endings of the scenes are usually dramatic, humorous, or both. Willy Russell is acutely aware of the need to grab the attention of the audience at the outset and then end on a powerful note, as if to carry over the momentum into the next scene. The end of this scene marks an important shift in attitude for Rita. Her admission that her mind is full of 'junk' and requires 'clearin' out' (p. 26) is evidence of a growing self-awareness.

SCENE 4 – A change in Rita

1. Rita is finding the course difficult, and this is made worse by a lack of support from Denny, her husband.

2. Rita's essay on Ibsen's *Peer Gynt* is only one line long – Frank provides her with the opportunity to re-write the esay.

When Rita comes on stage at the beginning of this scene, it is in stark contrast to her earlier entrances. As she walks into the room, she shuts the door and stands still, an unusual action considering her animated movements of the previous scenes. As she wrestles with her studies, in this case Forster's novel, her whole character begins to change and develop. Her mind freezes when contemplating Forster's phrase, 'only connect' (p. 26), which has her completely baffled. For the moment, however, Frank is more concerned with Rita's one-line response to an essay on Ibsen's *Peer Gynt*.

It is now that we learn that Rita, unsupported by her husband, does all her studying in the shop. Because the salon has been so busy during the week, Rita has been forced to encapsulate all her ideas into the briefest of responses. The conflict between home and studying becomes more apparent in this scene. Perhaps Denny realises that education will take Rita away from him. If so, it is **ironic** that, in not supporting his wife's studies, he creates an even bigger division between the two of them.

Frank tells Rita that, in an examination, there is a certain way of answering questions that is expected and, if she is to pass, then she must conform. Just as Rita conformed to expectations at school by not trying to succeed, she now has to conform to the expectations of examiners by adapting her style of language and the way she responds to texts. So, to allow her the opportunity of succeeding, Frank sets aside some time during the tutorial for Rita to write a more considered answer.

Sparked off by the thought of Peer Gynt's search for the meaning of life, Rita digresses about one of her customers who wished to do the same thing. She also adds that such a feeling is common to the working class, who appear to have lost their 'culture'. All she sees is 'everyone pissed, or on the Valium, tryin' to get from one day to the next' (p. 30). She likens it to a disease which no one dare mention and draws parallels with events in her own marriage. In identifying all these links, Frank points out that she is doing exactly what Forster was suggesting when he advised, 'only connect'.

DID YOU KNOW?

Just like Rita, Willy Russell also worked as a ladies' hairdresser in Liverpool before returning to education.

CHECKPOINT 15

What is Rita's view of 'working class culture'?

This is a valuable lesson for Rita and, along with the subsequent reasonable success of her *Peer Gynt* essay (at least, compared to her first attempt!), it strengthens the notion that, very gradually, she is becoming a 'proper' student.

Rita is being moulded and changed by Frank. Her character undergoes a major transformation, even to the extent of altering her natural speech. The language of the essay is not Rita's. Rather, it is the voice of a 'proper' student and, when we witness her success with the essay, we recognise that Rita is well on the way towards her ultimate goal.

CHECKPOINT 16

What example could you give to show how Rita is becoming increasingly conscious of her own use of language?

Now take a break!

WHO SAYS ...?

1 'you're a crazy mad piss artist who wants to throw his students through the window, an' I like you'

....

4 'everyone's pissed, or on the Valium, tryin' to get from one day to the next'

....

2 '...to wash away the memory of some silly woman's attempt to get into the mind of Henry James'

....

3 'My mind's full of junk'

....

ABOUT WHOM?

5 'It was about this old man who runs away from hospital an' goes out on the ale. He gets pissed an' stands in the street shoutin' an' challengin' death to come out an' fight. It's dead good'

....

6 'Haven't y' read it? It's a fantastic book. D' y' wanna lend it?'

....

7 'It's crap because the feller who wrote it was a louse'

....

8 'Do it on the radio'

....

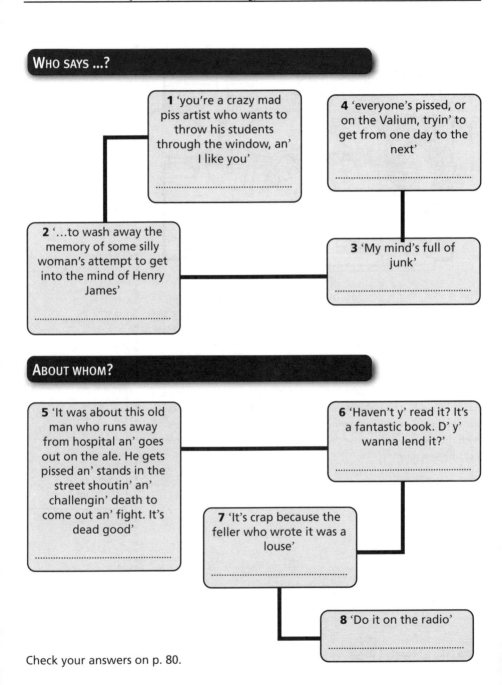

Check your answers on p. 80.

SCENE 5 – Denny burns the books

1 Rita reveals that Denny has burned her books in anger.

2 Frank gives Rita the opportunity to end the course.

3 The audience is given a deeper insight into Frank's drink problem and his inability to write poetry any more.

Rita's problems at home are intensified when we learn that Denny has burned all her books after finding that she was taking contraceptive pills again. She states that it is as if she was having an affair, although all she is doing is 'findin' meself' (p. 33). Rita recognises that this is the root of her marital crisis. She has changed and left Denny 'wonderin' where the girl he married has gone to' (p. 33).

 DID YOU KNOW?

The burning of books is seen in most cultures as an act of intellectual vandalism – both historically, as in 1930s Nazi Germany, and in Literature, as in Ray Bradbury's *Fahrenheit 451*.

The audience senses that the turning point for Rita is when Frank asks her whether she wants to discontinue the course. There is no hesitation in her reply, 'No. No!' (p. 34) and rather than discussing her marriage problems, it is significant that Rita chooses to talk about Chekhov instead. It is literature, she claims, which gives her life.

When he searches for the play on the top shelf, Frank discovers a bottle of whisky which he brings down and pours for himself and

Rita. His drink problem is known about by his employers, but, Frank says, they turn a blind eye to it so long as Frank is discreet and takes care to hide the signs. His drinking has become heavier since he ceased writing poetry, and when he is pressed by Rita, he confides that he stopped because he 'got it wrong' (p. 35). Instead of creating poetry, he was trying to create literature.

Frank admits that he stopped writing poetry because of a lack of inspiration, but he is also critical of his poetic style. His poetry was so finely crafted and academic in its style that it was almost devoid of real life. Because he has spent all his life in university circles, mixing with academics all the time, his writing became rather dry and intellectual.

There is a clear parallel to be drawn between Frank's criticism of his own poetry and the way he is attempting to educate Rita. Just as his poetry is emotionally barren, so he is pushing Rita in the same direction. The more educated she becomes, the less flamboyant is her language and behaviour. Instead of responding to texts naturally and with honesty from the heart, she learns to use her mind to analyse them in a rather cold and characterless fashion. It would appear that to succeed in the academic world, it is necessary for Rita to curb her lively ways and be transformed into a 'proper' student.

The scene ends with Rita persuading Frank to visit an amateur production of *The Importance of Being Earnest*.

CHECKPOINT 17
What are the possible reasons for Frank's heavy drinking?

DID YOU KNOW?

Theatre can help your studies! Like Rita, take an interest in what's on at your local theatres. In particular, it will aid your study of *Educating Rita* if you can see it in performance.

Scene 6 – Rita has seen *Macbeth*

❶ Rita talks excitedly about her visit to the theatre.

❷ During the scene, Rita realises that she has left a customer under a hair dryer.

Frank's moment of relaxation at the beginning of this scene is quickly shattered when Rita bursts through the door in a state of intense excitement, after visiting a professional theatre the night before. She is desperate to talk about the play, *Macbeth*, but finds it difficult to express her ideas: 'Wasn't his wife a cow, eh?' (p. 40).

If the audience had begun to accept that Rita was well on the route to academic success, then they are allowed to see her limitations at first hand when she discusses *Macbeth* with Frank.

Rita's lack of a critical, academic vocabulary is not her only limitation at this time. In terms of literary concepts, she demonstrates her lack of knowledge when discussing the notion of tragedy. Rita responds to literature from the heart. Whereas Frank is critical and detached, Rita becomes involved and engaged with the characters on stage, almost to the point of shouting out loud to warn Macbeth of his impending doom.

Frank discusses the concept of **tragedy** with Rita, as opposed to something which is tragic. Rita invites Frank to an art gallery the next day and the scene ends with Frank's invitation to Rita to attend a dinner party organised by his partner, Julia. Denny is also invited but Rita suspects that he will not go. Her lack of confidence is expressed by her final question, 'What shall I wear?' (p. 42). Rita's lack of confidence in accepting Frank's invitation has links with the next scene where we find that Rita has been unable to attend the party through fear of making a fool of herself, whether it be to do with wearing the wrong clothes, saying the wrong things or even taking the wrong wine. Her metamorphosis into a confident, educated woman is far from complete.

Throughout the play, however, Rita demonstrates a certain amount of self-awareness. Looking out of the window, she sees the other students who she is desperately trying to emulate and recognises that she is not yet one of them.

There is a constant thread of humour running throughout the play. Note how Rita's language is, once again, the source of much comedy in the play. When she suddenly remembers that she should have been back at work a long time ago, her reaction is typical: 'Christ – me customer. She only wanted a demi-wave – she'll come out looking like a friggin' muppet' (p. 42).

? DID YOU KNOW?
Aristotle was a Greek philosopher who, among other things, first developed the concept of tragedy in the *Ars Poetica*.

CHECKPOINT 18
Why does Frank invite Rita to the dinner party?

Scene 7 – Rita fails to make the dinner party

❶ Rita explains why she could not bring herself to attend the dinner party.

❷ Rita desribes her Saturday evening in the pub with her family.

CHECKPOINT 19

Why couldn't Rita pluck up the courage to go in to the dinner party?

This is a pivotal scene in Rita's development. Having been unable to pluck up the confidence or courage to cross over the threshold at Frank's dinner party, she now comes to explain why. One of Rita's concerns was that she might have brought the wrong type of wine. Here again, Willy Russell undercuts the seriousness of the situation with his humour. 'It wouldn't have mattered if you'd walked in with a bottle of Spanish plonk' says Frank. 'It was Spanish' comes the reply (p. 44).

Frank asks Rita why she simply couldn't be herself, and she admits that it's because she doesn't want to be 'myself' (p. 45). She wants to become a different person, but at this stage of the play she is trapped between two worlds, a 'half-caste' (p. 45) as she describes herself. She is uncomfortable with the people she lives with and yet does not fit in with Frank's world either.

CHECKPOINT 20

Why does Rita describe herself as a 'half-caste'?

The invitation to dinner was partly a **symbolic** act. To attend the function would signify acceptance in Frank's social circle, and yet Rita knows that she is not ready for the transition from her world into that of Frank. She fails to do it at this stage because she knows in her heart that she does not possess the language, the knowledge or the style of the middle-class academics to whom she aspires.

It is interesting to note that Frank describes Rita's character as 'funny, delightful, charming' (p. 44) but Rita, herself, rejects his attempts to compliment her as being patronising. She does not want to be funny but wants to 'talk seriously with the rest of you' (p. 44). Spurred on by this desire, Rita's metamorphosis gathers momentum.

Initially, her reaction was to stop visiting Frank's tutorials and get on with her life. However, on going back to the pub where her family are enjoying a Saturday night sing-song, she sees her mother crying. When she asks her why, her mother replies 'because we could sing better songs than those' (p. 46). Rita recognises the significance of this comment immediately. Just like her mother, Rita is **metaphorically** searching for a new 'song' to sing, and that is why she eventually decides to carry on with her education.

CHECKPOINT 21

What happens in the pub and why is it a turning point in Rita's development?

A turning point for Rita

The Saturday night that Rita spends in the pub with her family is a turning point in her development. It comes on the same evening that Rita has been unable to bring herself to go to Frank's and Julia's dinner party. Rita feels trapped between two conflicting worlds and famously describes herself as a 'half-caste' who neither fits in with Denny's working-class culture, nor with Frank's respectable world of middle-class academics.

It is only later in the scene, at the pub, that Rita realises that she only has one option in her life, namely to throw herself wholeheartedly into her studies. When she notices that her mother is crying, Rita takes the decision that she will never end up like her mother who clearly feels unfulfilled in life. For Rita, education now represents a route out of her working-class background and away from a life of drudgery.

The play sets up the contrast between this working-class culture as opposed to the culture of the middle class, who are seen to entertain themselves at dinner parties or at the theatre.

The act of Rita's mother crying has a **metaphorical** significance. Denny gets her laughing again and, because we have made the connection between Rita and her mother who are both dissatisfied with their lives, we are forced to consider the logical argument that the same could happen to Rita. The laughter could very easily cover the pain which exists just below the surface.

SCENE 8 – Rita leaves Denny

1 Rita arrives at Frank's room with her suitcase, having left her husband.

2 Despite her problems, Rita wants to carry on as normal.

3 Frank and Rita discuss her essay on *Macbeth*.

Rita tells Frank how Denny has given her the ultimatum: either stop studying and come off the pill or leave altogether. Having chosen the latter, she turns up at Frank's room with her suitcase. Rita has arranged to spend some time with her mother until she can find a flat of her own.

CHECKPOINT 22

How does Rita react to the end of her marriage?

Under the circumstances, Frank is finding it difficult to carry on 'business as usual' and is reticent about criticising one of Rita's essays. Yet Rita wants to discuss her *Macbeth* essay, rather than dwelling on her home troubles with Denny, in a similar way that she wanted to talk about Chekhov and Frank tried to get her to forget studies and focus on what was happening in her life in Scene 5. Frank therefore discusses Rita's essay, telling her that it is 'totally honest' and 'moving' (p. 47), but in terms of helping her pass exams it is 'worthless' (p. 48). Rita asks how to go about changing this, but Frank states he does not know if he can do this as he will have to change her. However, Rita is adamant that she wants to change and she needs Frank to help in her education, even if it means abandoning her 'uniqueness' (p. 48).

Rita's strength and determination shine through when, at the end of the scene, the curtain closes with her tearing up the essay, dumping it in the bin and preparing to 'start again' (p. 48).

Note how Rita's changing character is causing her to leave 'Susan' further and further behind. The dissolution of her marriage is the last tie with her former life and Rita is now free to develop as she pleases. Any sadness or sympathy we feel for Denny disappears when we consider the way he has restricted her intellectual growth. In addition, there is also the notion that he, too, is a free agent once again and that he will undoubtedly find another wife, and probably someone who is more suited to his lifestyle and his desire for children.

When Frank tells Rita that, for her to succeed, she may have to abandon her 'uniqueness' (p. 48), he is recognising that to change Rita's entire being may not necessarily be a wholly positive achievement. Having witnessed the destruction of her marriage as a direct result of her education, he is rightly concerned that, instead of finding herself, she may in fact be losing her true identity. Furthermore, it is apparent to Frank that in training Rita to quell her vibrant character and write from the head rather than the heart, he is actually negating all those features which attracted him to Rita in the first place.

 DID YOU KNOW?

Rita enrolled on one of the courses run by the Open University. The OU is now one of the largest providers of education in the country, providing a range of different types of course. It is likely that Rita would now study Literature as part of a distance learning package so she might never have met Frank!

Scene 8 continued

DID YOU KNOW?

Russell once said: 'when making *Educating Rita* I tried very hard to write a love story'.

This is a crucial scene which encapsulates Rita's personality, aims and desires, and is a highly dramatic way of bringing this first act to an end. Rita's determination to change prepares us for Act II.

Now take a break!

Who says ...?

1 'Christ – me customer. She only wanted a demi-wave – she'll come out looking like a friggin' muppet'

....

2 'It wouldn't have mattered if you'd walked in with a bottle of Spanish plonk'

....

About whom?

3 'I see him lookin' at me sometimes, an' I know what he's thinkin', I do y' know, he's wonderin' where the girl he married has gone to'

....

4 'If she knew I was at the theatre with an irresistible thing like you? Rita, it would be deaf and dumb breakfasts for a week'

....

6 'An' she was cryin', but no one could get it out of her why she was cryin'. Everyone just said she was pissed an' we should get her home'

....

5 'You see he goes blindly on and on and with every step he's spinning one more piece of thread which will eventually make up the network of his own tragedy'

....

Check your answers on p. 80.

SCENE 1 – Rita returns from summer school

① Rita tells of her time at summer school.

② Frank tries to introduce a new poet to Rita but she has already 'done' William Blake.

CHECKPOINT 23

How does Rita's entrance at the start of Act 2 differ from her entrance in the opening scene of the play?

A significant amount of time has elapsed since Act I. Frank has, once again, begun to write poetry and, when Rita enters, she is a different Rita, bursting through the door as usual but this time dressed in new second-hand clothes which she displays for Frank in the form of a twirl.

Rita's success at summer school means that she is brimming with confidence. She has stopped smoking, moved in with a new flatmate called Trish and, as she admits, 'I'm havin' the time of me life' (p. 51).

The new Rita

Following her success at summer school, a new Rita has begun to emerge. Above all, what Rita has gained from her recent course is a newly found self-confidence that manifests itself through her new clothes, the way she speaks and the new friends she has made.

Just as Rita becomes more confident and receives a much-needed boost to her self-esteem, Frank's own sense of importance begins to diminish. When Rita breaks the news to Frank that she has already 'done' William Blake at summer school, it represents a significant shift in their relationship because, for the first time, Rita has not been reliant on Frank for her learning. The audience witnesses Frank, who had excitedly taken a volume of Blake's poetry down from the bookcase, return the book with an air of resignation. Once she has started down the road to independence, Rita will need less and less support from Frank.

Frank, on the other hand, is having a bad time of it. Julia has left him during the summer and, although she has now returned, Frank is still drinking heavily.

Moreover, Rita's present of a pen with the inscription, 'Must only be used for poetry' (p. 52) only serves as a further reminder of his own creative failings. Rita is attempting to reform him, but Frank knows only too well that Rita's influence is a temporary measure and that, like all students, her leaving is inevitable.

To change the mood, Frank tries to introduce Rita to the work of a 'new' poet but he is surprised to learn that she has already 'done' William Blake at summer school. Rita recites a poem from memory and explains that even though Blake was not on the syllabus, one of her tutors was such a 'Blake freak' (p. 55) that she ended up reading his works anyway.

Rita's changing language is instantly recognisable. When she tells Frank about her conversation with the tutor who asked her whether she was fond of Ferlinghetti, Rita acknowledges that the old Rita would have said 'only with Parmesan cheese' (p. 50). Instead, her reply is a carefully controlled and serious response: 'Actually I'm

 DID YOU KNOW?

William Blake (1757–1827) was a visionary poet, printmaker and artist who believed the imagination to be man's most important faculty.

CHECKPOINT 24

What are the main differences in Rita's character before and after the interval?

CHECK THE BOOK

William Blake's *Songs of Innocence and of Experience* would be a good introduction to his poetry. Why does Rita feel so strongly about his work?

CHECKPOINT 25

How does the audience's perception of Frank begin to change in this scene?

---

not too familiar with the American poets.' (p. 50). She also uses words like **analogy**, **parody** and **tragedy** with apparent ease, in contrast to not knowing what **assonance** meant at the beginning of Act I. Note, also, how she is beginning to echo the words of Trish, her flatmate, when stating that 'A room is like a plant' (p. 53).

Frank is being stifled by his lecturer's role in the university. It offers little creativity and gives him no satisfaction. On top of this, his relationship with Julia seems to have stagnated. Rita senses this, wanting to throw open the windows and bring new life to Frank's room.

With Rita's newly acquired confidence and intellectual maturity, we detect a subtle shift in the balance of their relationship. Frank's relevance to Rita is not quite what it was at the beginning of her education. For example, her assertion that she had already 'done' Blake at summer school is the first occasion when Rita surprises Frank with her literary knowledge. Putting the book back on the shelf is significant, indicating that, for once, Frank has fallen out of step with Rita's education. The fact that she developed good relationships with other tutors on the course means the beginning of a sense of insecurity and even jealousy for Frank.

Scene 2 – Rita becomes a 'proper' student

1. Rita puts on an affected voice.

2. Rita tells of plucking up courage to sit on the grass with the 'proper' students.

3. Frank learns that Rita has been invited to the South of France with some of the other students.

Arriving late for her tutorial, Rita begins by speaking with an affected voice which she sees as 'talking properly' (p. 57). Her flatmate, Trish, has told her that 'there is not a lot of point in discussing beautiful literature in an ugly voice' (p. 56), but Frank is quick to point out that she hasn't got an ugly voice, or at least she didn't have. He tells her to be herself but, as Rita indicated earlier in the play she is trying to become educated because 'I don't want to be myself' (p. 45). Trish is becoming another influence in her life. She is a different form of teacher and becomes a sort of role model for Rita.

Continuing from her success at the summer school and her growing confidence which has resulted in her changing character, we now learn that for the first time, Rita has actually mixed with the 'proper' students and she has quickly realised that they are not so infallible after all. Her illusions of their academic prowess are shattered as she wins her argument with the other students about D.H. Lawrence. This represents a shift in her attitude and confidence. Rita is now able to hold her own in academic circles, whether it be down on the lawns below Frank's window or in a more formal manner at the summer school.

CHECKPOINT 26

What is significant about Rita going to sit on the grass with the other students?

Rita reports that one of the students, nicknamed Tiger, has invited her on a Christmas vacation to the south of France with the rest of his crowd. Frank reacts with what appears to be jealousy, making excuses about why she would be unable to go. Rita is shocked and cuts Frank short, suggesting that he is being ridiculous. The scene ends, however, with Frank returning one of Rita's essays, telling her that it 'wouldn't look out of place' (p. 59) with the work of the other students on his desk.

CHECKPOINT 27

What evidence is there to suggest that the relationship between Frank and Rita is starting to break down?

Placing the essay on top of the pile is **symbolic**. Rita has finally 'made it'. No longer is she out of place, and no longer can she describe herself as a 'half-caste' (p. 45).

SCENE 3 – Frank hits the bottle

1 **Frank tells how his drinking has got him into trouble with the university authorities.**

2 **Rita and Frank argue.**

CHECKPOINT 28

What is unusual about the opening of this scene?

The lights come up on Rita, and it is Frank who is very drunk that makes the dramatic, if rather clumsy entrance. He has been reported by some students for being drunk and falling off the rostrum when delivering a lecture. The university authorities have stopped short of giving Frank the sack, but he is being forced to take a sabbatical somewhere abroad for a year or so, presumably to get him out of the way.

Frank reveals his feelings of discontent towards his regular students when describing them as 'a crowd of mealy-mouthed pricks who wouldn't know a poet if you beat them about the head with one' (p. 60). In his lecture, he has quoted Rita's line from earlier in the play: 'Assonance means getting the rhyme wrong' (p. 60). Rather understandably, the students were disdainful for they did not share Frank's understanding of the line. Out of context, it sounds ridiculous.

Note how Frank is lapsing into Rita's language, using the phrase 'Completely off my cake' (p. 60). He also swears at the start of the scene, uses her original definitions of literary terms like **assonance**, and is even reading the books she read, reminiscent of Rita at the beginning of the play.

Rita is ready to postpone the tutorial until the following week, but Frank engages her in a conversation about her essay on William Blake. He concedes that if it were written in an examination it would earn a high grade, but he dislikes it because it is too impersonal. Rita complains that, in the beginning, Frank had urged her to write in this objective style. By educating Rita, Frank changes her, but he also wants to retain the old Rita. The more she develops, the less she reminds him of the 'girl' who walked through his door and brought a 'breath of air' (p. 11) to his life. **Ironically**, this is akin to Denny's reaction in the first half of the play when he, too, wondered where the 'girl' he married had gone to.

The dialogue develops into an argument with Rita confirming that she no longer needs Frank as much as she used to when she first started attending his classes and it is seemingly inevitable that their relationship will break down. Frank had always perceived that Rita would only need him for a short time before she was able to exist independently, but this does not lessen the blow for him. Once again, just like Denny who precipitated the marriage breakdown, Frank's petulant behaviour only serves to create further problems with Rita.

The scene ends on a lighter, if not ironic, note with Frank stating that he had read *Rubyfruit Jungle* and liked it, a book Rita had referred to in Act I, Scene 1.

CHECKPOINT 29

Why is Frank critical of Rita's development?

Now take a break!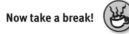

Test yourself (Act II, scenes 1–3)

Who says …?

1 'there is not a lot of point in discussing beautiful literature in an ugly voice'

....

4 'A room is like a plant'

....

2 'I'm havin' the time of me life'

....

3 'Actually I'm not too familiar with the American poets'

....

About whom?

5 'She's great. Y' know she's dead classy. Y' know like, she's got taste …'

....

8 'Or maybe they did it because they're a crowd of mealy-mouthed pricks who wouldn't know a poet if you beat them about the head with one'

....

6 'There was this really mad one with them; I've only been talkin' to them for five minutes and he's inviting me to go abroad with them all'

....

7 'They suggested a sabbatical for a year – or ten … Europe – or America … I suggested that Austrialia might be more apt – the allusion was lost on them …'

....

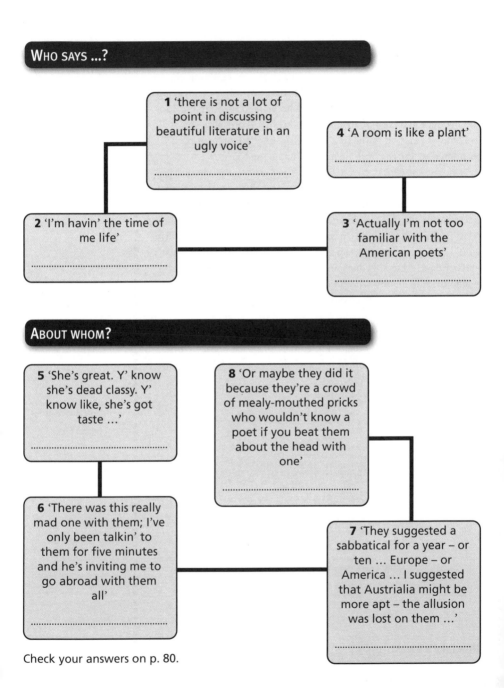

Check your answers on p. 80.

SCENE 4 – Rita changes jobs

1 Frank's drinking becomes worse.

2 Frank seems jealous of Tiger and fearful of 'losing' Rita.

3 Rita is given Frank's poetry to analyse.

Because Rita is late for her tutorial, Frank rings the hairdresser's shop only to find that she has left her job. She now works in a bistro. When questioning Rita about why she has done this, and why she hasn't told him, she says she is fed up of talking about 'irrelevant rubbish' (p. 64) and she is now able to talk 'about what's important' (p. 65). The change in jobs is part of Rita's metamorphosis into an entirely different character. Just like changing her name and trying to alter the sound of her own voice, it reflects a desire to put her previous existence firmly in the past.

Frank asks whether Mr Tyson, or Tiger as he is known to his friends, is one of Rita's customers at the bistro. She admits that he is and that she finds him and the other students fascinating. She enjoys being in their company because they are so full of life. Frank's apparent jealousy over Tiger makes him seem insecure and almost like a schoolboy. The reason, presumably, is that Frank feels that he is 'losing' Rita. When he says, 'perhaps you don't want to waste your time coming here anymore?' (p. 65), he cuts a rather pathetic figure, wallowing in his own misery. Drink, however, clearly plays a part in this scene and accentuates Frank's reactions.

Frank asks Rita whether she can be bothered to attend the classes any more and suggests that she now dislikes spending any amount of time there. Rita's reply is emphatic: 'For God's sake, I don't want to stop coming here. I've got to come here. What about my exam?' (p. 65).

Throughout the scene, Frank is pouring whisky down his throat and Rita is blunt when telling him that if he stopped drinking, he 'might be able to talk about things that matter instead of where I do or don't work; an' then it might be worth comin' here' (p. 66).

 DID YOU KNOW?
The character of Rita was played in the original West End stage production by Julie Walters, who also went on to star in the film version of the play.

CHECKPOINT 30

What are Frank's reasons for giving Rita the poems to analyse?

In an attempt to test whether Rita does or does not know what 'matters', Frank hands her some of his own poetry, asking for a critical, non-subjective and non-sentimental appraisal by the following week. Asking Rita to criticise his poetry is Frank's idea of a 'test', not in the conventional sense, but in the sense that it will clarify whether or not Rita has lost the ability to respond openly and honestly. He is afraid that she has become cold and subjective like the rest of his students whom he despises so much.

Scene 5 – Rita gives her view of Frank's poetry

1 **Rita is full of praise for Frank's poetry.**

2 **Frank dismisses Rita and her opinions as worthless.**

3 **Their relationship is breaking down.**

CHECK THE BOOK

Mary Shelley's *Frankenstein* is worth reading, if only to compare how Hollywood has treated the story in a variety of films. How does Frank compare with Frankenstein who created a 'monster'?

Having sat up late with her flatmate, Trish, to read Frank's poems, Rita returns the following day to his room at the university, full of praise for his work. She describes the poems as 'brilliant', 'witty', 'profound' and 'full of style' (p. 67), but Frank's view is in stark contrast: 'this clever, pyrotechnical pile of self-conscious allusion is worthless, talentless shit and should be recognized as such by anyone with a shred of common sense' (p. 68). He makes the point that Rita, when she first started her visits, would have said exactly the same. He feels that like Mary Shelley, writer of *Frankenstein*, he has created his own 'monster'. He recognises that the Rita who first brought that 'breath of air' (p. 11) into his room has gone for ever. In describing the poems as 'pretentious, characterless and without style' (p. 68), he is suggesting that the new Rita who admires them so much must possess these same qualities.

Leaving the room after being insulted, Rita tells Frank that she no longer needs him because she is now educated with a 'room full of books' (p. 68). She now knows 'what clothes to wear' and 'what wine to buy, what plays to see, what papers and books to read' (p. 68). Frank sees this as worthless and asks Rita, 'Found a culture have you Rita? Found a better song to sing have you?' (p. 69). He is referring to the night when Rita is in the pub and she spots her mother crying. The 'song' represents an alternative and better lifestyle. Frank, however, is not convinced that Rita has found anything better or that her newly found culture is any better than her past.

As she leaves, he calls her 'Rita' and she laughs in his face. She says that no-one calls her 'Rita' any more but him and that she 'dropped' the name when she realised it was 'pretentious crap' (p. 69).

The change of name seals the metamorphosis of Rita's character. Instead of playing at being different, Rita has finally found her true self. She no longer needs to hide behind a new name and accepts that she is Susan. Frank's name-calling, unfortunately, suggests that he feels Rita has still not 'found herself'.

CHECKPOINT 31

Why has Rita reverted back to her real name of Susan, and why does Frank continue to call her Rita?

SCENE 6 – Frank rings the bistro

❶ **Time has elapsed and Frank is calling Rita/Susan to remind her of the examination.**

This short scene begins with Frank's telephone call to the bistro in order to inform Rita that she has been entered for her examination.

CHECKPOINT 32

Think about Frank's reasons for ringing Rita. Why do you think he calls her?

Initially, he asks for Rita but quickly realises his mistake and changes the name to Susan. As she is not there, he is forced to hang up. There is a black-out to denote the passing of time and when the lights come up again he is talking to Trish over the phone, giving her details of the examination to pass on to Rita. Here, again, he cannot become accustomed to calling her 'Susan': 'Erm, yes I'm a friend of Rita's ... Rita ... I'm sorry Susan' (p. 69).

The telephone calls show that, since his last meeting with Rita, Frank has had time to consider his words and actions, and has come to the realisation that Rita should at least have the opportunity of sitting her examination.

Frank is unable to accept the change of name because it represents the change in character. As she arrived with the name of Rita, Frank will always associate it with the 'breath of air' (p. 11) which swept into his room on the night of her first tutorial.

SCENE 7 – Rita has passed but Frank is leaving

1 Frank is leaving for Australia.

2 A new, confident 'Rita' emerges.

3 Frank gives Rita the present of the dress.

The final scene opens with Rita, smoking again and wearing a large winter coat to illustrate that time has, once again, moved on. It is now close to Christmas and Rita has passed her examination. She is returning to thank Frank for being a good teacher and is surprised to find him packing his belongings into several tea-chests.

Lighting a cigarette marks a partial return to Rita's old ways. In this scene we have evidence that Rita, or Susan as she is now known again, has matured into a confident and articulate woman who is finally at ease with herself. Even her language, although less rough around the edges, is more like her speech at the start of the play. No longer does she feel it necessary to change her voice, she can simply be herself.

The university authorities have been forced to respond to Frank's drink problem and, rather than sacking him, they are sending him away to Australia for two years. He tries to make light of it when joking that the Australians named their favourite drink after a literary figure: 'Forster's Lager they call it' (p. 71). When talking about 'Forster's (rather than Foster's) Lager', Frank is referring to Rita's early error over the spelling of E.M. Forster's name. Note how this comes about in the form of gentle teasing. It is noticeable that the warmth and light-hearted way of talking has returned to their relationship. However, the laughter only just covers the pain he is undoubtedly going through. Julia is not going with him and this, effectively, means the end of their relationship.

Rita tells Frank about the question on *Peer Gynt* in her examination which was the same as the one set by Frank in one of her early tutorials. Earlier she simply wrote 'Do it on the radio' (p. 72) and Frank was critical. Now, she suspects that Frank would have been proud of her if she had responded in this way. It seems as though part of her wanted to, but she chose not to, and that ability to choose is the most important gift that Frank has been able to bestow on Rita. She also tells him about Trish, who was her model and teacher, trying to 'top herself'.

Rita evades Frank's invitation to go to Australia and tells him that she's already been invited to the south of France with Tiger and his

> **CHECKPOINT 33**
>
> Why is Frank packing his belongings away at the start of this scene?

> **GLOSSARY**
>
> **Foster's Lager** a well-known brand of Australian lager, but Frank is jokingly referring to Rita's early confusion over the names when reading the work of E.M. Forster

Scene 7 continued

CHECKPOINT 34

What has Rita gained and what has she lost as a result of her education?

friends and to her mother's for Christmas. When Frank asks what she will do, she replies, 'I dunno. I might go to France. I might go to me mother's. I might even have a baby. I dunno. I'll make a decision. I'll choose' (pp. 72–3).

What the future holds

For both Frank and Rita, the future is full of uncertainty and excitement. Frank is packing his belongings into several tea-chests bound for Australia. His enforced sabbatical has been designed so that the University authorities do not have to take stronger action against his heavy drinking and his embarrassing antics in front of the students, and the audience recognises that this gives him the chance of a fresh start. The fact that he is going to the 'New World' country of Australia suggests that he is beginning a more hopeful chapter in his life and that a new environment will lead to a moderation in his drinking, a renewed poetic creativity and maybe even some sense of personal fulfilment in his private life.

For Rita, the future is by no means certain. Her recent education has given her the prospect of a new job, new friends, a new home and the chance to travel but, at the end of the play Rita confirms that, above all else, education has finally provided her with the ability to choose her own destiny rather than having her whole life mapped out by others, and it is this that she savours: 'I might go to France. I might go to me mother's. I might even have a baby. I dunno. I'll make a decision. I'll choose' (pp. 72–3).

Frank gives Rita a present of a dress, which refers to earlier in the play when Rita refused to buy a new dress until she passed her first examination. Frank's love for Rita, possibly suggested by his jealousy earlier in the play, now becomes evident as he shows that he has remembered her words and acted with tenderness in buying the gift.

Rita says that she feels that all she has ever done is to take things from Frank. However, here, at the very end of the play there are distinctly sexual overtones, when Rita suggests that there is one thing that she can do for him to say thank you for all his teaching. In a moment of comic genius, Willy Russell has Rita undercut the tension of the scene by taking out a pair of scissors to trim Frank's hair. Grabbing a pair of scissors from the desk, she prepares to cut his hair with the closing line, 'I'm gonna take ten years off you' (p. 73).

> **CHECKPOINT 35**
>
> What does the cutting of Frank's hair represent?

Now take a break!

Who says ...?

1 'It's the sort of thing that gives publishing a bad name. Wit? You'll find more wit in the telephone book'

....

4 'I'm gonna take ten years off you'

....

2 'For God's sake, I don't want to stop coming here. I've got to come here. What about my exam?'

....

3 'this clever, pyrotechnical pile of self-conscious allusion is worthless, talentless shit and should be recognized as such by anyone with a shred of common sense'

....

About whom?

5 'They're young, and they're passionate about things that matter. They're not trapped'

....

6 'She spends half her life eatin' wholefoods an' health foods to make her live longer, an' the other half tryin' to kill herself'

....

7 'I bought it some time ago – for erm – for an educated woman friend – of mine'

....

Check your answers on p. 80.

PART THREE

COMMENTARY

THEMES

PEOPLE AND ENVIRONMENT

Frank

With all the action taking place in Frank's study, we always see him in the middle of his own environment. The room is cluttered with books and his other belongings. Comfortable to the point of stagnation, it is only when Rita comes on the scene that the room has its 'first breath of air' (p. 11) for many years. Later in the play, she feels the need to throw open the window saying that 'A room is like a plant' (p. 53) and it needs air. This stifling, rather oppressive atmosphere could be one reason for Frank's lack of creativity. **Ironically**, at the end of the play, the audience senses that his imminent banishment to Australia could be just the thing to spark off some form of poetic inspiration.

Rita

Quite the opposite to Frank, Rita is cast into an alien environment right from the beginning and, initially, she appears to be like a fish out of water. Her accent and **dialect** compared with Frank's assured use of 'Standard English', and her working-class, non-academic background clearly set her apart from Frank's 'proper' students. The resultant lack of confidence causes Rita to baulk at going to Frank's dinner party because she knows that she doesn't fit in. Sadly, she also realises that, having outgrown her family and friends, she no longer belongs in her own class either. Describing herself as a 'freak' and a 'half-caste' (p. 45) who is stuck between two worlds, she realises that she must either turn the clock back and return to her former life, or press ahead with her education and become accepted in a new environment – the social circles inhabited by the other university students.

 DID YOU KNOW?
Although Willy Russell is renowned for his comedies, there is usually a darker side to his writing, based in critical social commentary.

INCOMPLETENESS

In terms of their characters, both Frank and Rita show an alarming sense of incompleteness.

Rita

Rita, in particular, is driven by the need for education, having realised that life has more to offer than her mundane existence in a hairdressing salon. At the age of twenty-six she feels 'out of step' (p. 12) and tells Frank that, before considering having a baby with Denny, she would need to discover herself first. Ultimately, this costs Rita her marriage, her friends and her job.

Although Frank suggests that her education results merely in her singing 'a different song' (p. 69), rather than achieving a necessarily better life, the Rita at the end of the play is a whole, rounded character, who possesses the knowledge, skills and confidence to choose her own direction in life.

Frank

Frank, too, has something lacking in his life. His rather jaded outlook not only results in poor teaching for the majority of his students, but it also blocks his poetic creativity. Already divorced from his wife, his relationship with Julia does not appear set to last and he seeks comfort from all his problems in the form of a whisky bottle. Unlike Rita, he fails to attain a sense of completeness in the play. However, the prospect of a new life in Australia, where things are 'just beginning' (p. 72) does at least offer some hope for the future.

Rita's family

Just like Frank, Rita's family all seek to escape from their problems through alcohol. The Saturday night sing-song in the local pub is suggestive of happiness and family unity, but the reality of the situation is very different. Their laughter and song is a thin veil which covers up the painful knowledge that their lives are unfulfilled and incomplete. Rita's mother shows that she has achieved this state of self-knowledge when she cries, saying that they could all be singing 'better songs than those' (p. 46).

CHECKPOINT 36

Instead of considering Frank's banishment as a punishment, how easy is it to view his trip to Australia as a liberation?

METAMORPHOSIS

Rita's education is much more than simply learning about English Literature. It represents a complete change in her being. As Frank tells Rita, for her to pass the examination, she must suppress or even abandon her 'uniqueness'. 'You're going to have to change' (p. 48), he says. Her lively, irrepressible nature is suppressed and even her language undergoes a transformation, causing Frank finally to regret the way he has changed her. In doing so, he compares himself to Mary Shelley (p. 68), the author of *Frankenstein*, because he also feels that he has created a 'monster'.

The metamorphosis is a slow and painful process for Rita. Halfway through, she likens herself to a 'half-caste' (p. 45), who is both out of place in her own society and yet unable to fit into Frank's social circles too. The change of name from Susan to Rita is significant, but in attempting to create a new identity, Rita inevitably makes mistakes. She is taken in by the vitality of Tiger and the other students and treats her flatmate, Trish, with reverence. However, by the end of the play, Rita has seen the truth. Trish, having survived a suicide attempt, is seen as neurotic and fragile, while Tiger is simply 'a bit of a wanker really' (p. 72). And, as if to seal the change and acceptance of her character, she reverts back to her original name.

Thus, Rita emerges from her metamorphosis as a whole, more rounded character. Gone is the affected language, and along with the return of her natural speech comes the re-establishing of her vibrant sense of humour. She has matured and, **symbolically**, Frank's present of the dress serves to emphasis this fact.

EDUCATION

Rita finds herself on an Open University course as a direct result of her failure at school where studying was 'just for the whimps' (p. 17). She acknowledges that if she had taken school seriously, she would have become different to her friends.

Having broken free, to some extent, from that kind of peer pressure, Rita's second attempt at education shows her to be an enthusiastic and highly motivated student. She has an idealised vision of 'proper'

CHECK THE BOOK

See how Willy Russell treats a similar theme in the form of his novel, *The Wrong Boy*.

CHECKPOINT 37

What 'mistakes' does Rita make on her journey to education?

CHECKPOINT 38

What are Frank's strengths and weaknesses as a teacher?

students, to which she feels she does not belong. Frank's description of his students is in stark contrast. 'Proper students don't read and study' (p. 16), he tells Rita. They are 'appalling' scholars who 'wouldn't know a poet if you beat them about the head with one' (p. 60).

Because her desire to change her direction in life sets her apart from the other students, Frank is placed under pressure. Rita wants to learn 'everything' and Frank appears to baulk at the challenge. For the majority of the time, his 'appalling teaching', as he describes it, is 'quite in order for most of my appalling students' (p. 13), but Frank knows that Rita deserves better. Rita declines his offer to find another tutor, sensing that their compatibility will be all-important, and it is the strength of their relationship which enables Rita to develop into an excellent student.

For Rita, education is a way out of an unfulfilling lifestyle. In the final scene, after she has passed her examination, she recognises that it may well have all been worthless in the end, meaning that it may not radically alter her life, but at least she now has some element of choice in her life. She does not mean the type of choices open to her husband, Denny, such as choosing between the eight different kinds of lager in the pub, but real choices which can affect the direction of her life. She has the opportunity to make a fresh start in Australia with Frank, she could carry on working in the bistro, she could return to her old job as a hairdresser, or she could choose to do something completely different.

STRUCTURE

The play is **structured** in two Acts and is perfectly balanced. The first half deals with Rita's struggle to fit into Frank's world. He is the one who is seen to be in control. He possesses all the knowledge and speaks the right words. Rita, on the other hand, is exactly the opposite in the sense that she struggles with language in the beginning, only developing the necessary skills to succeed in Act II, after her success at the summer school.

Just as the first half of the play sees the breakdown of Rita's marriage, the second half contains evidence of a rift between Frank and Julia. Act I witnesses Rita's gradual development to the point where she fits in, whereas Act II reflects Frank's growing alienation from the world of the academics, eventually resulting in his banishment to Australia. The great **antithesis** in the play is the fact that the more Rita is educated, the less she needs Frank, and the more this leads to a relationship of conflict.

The interval is a 'hinge'. After the interval and her success on the summer school course, Rita seems to be a changed character. Rita now appears to be the one beginning to take charge of the proceedings, and Frank's attempts to select a poet for study backfire on him, when Rita announces that she has already analysed Blake's poetry on her summer course. Frank becomes the character who is having problems, while Rita goes from strength to strength.

The concluding scenes of the play reflect the increasing sense of pace. They become shorter and there is the undoubted feeling that time has elapsed in the build up towards Rita's examination.

The play is **naturalistic** in its **setting**. The one set allows all the action to take place inside Frank's room and, by adhering to the **unity** of place, Willy Russell is able to concentrate both on the drama and the humour of the play.

CHARACTERS

RITA

Initially, Rita is out of place in the middle-class world of the academics. Her language is coarse and vulgar, and she does not possess the vocabulary to express literary concepts on anything other than a basic level. When she passes on the opportunity of attending Frank's dinner party, she does so because she knows that she will feel out of place in those surroundings. She is preoccupied by wearing the right clothes and by taking the correct type of wine, as well as worrying about saying the right things.

As a student, Rita does not possess the self-confidence of those people who attend his regular lectures. Failure at school the first

At first:
Common
Uneducated
Humorous

Finally:
Confident
Mature
Humorous

time round has meant that Rita has developed an idealised vision of university education. She does not want to go down on the lawn below Frank's window because she feels inferior.

CHECK THE FILM
Shirley Valentine stars Pauline Collins in the title role. What similarities and differences can you find between the characters of Rita and Shirley?

Almost inevitably, the first half of the play charts the problems encountered by Rita in her married life with Denny. Her education, it seems, takes her away from her family and friends into an entirely new sphere of life. Her husband wants her to have children and yet Rita knows that before she has a baby, she needs to get to know herself. She deceives Denny by taking the contraceptive pill against his will, and knows how the disintegration of their relationship is affecting him. In return, Denny's refusal to support Rita in her education not only causes problems for her, but it probably hastens the demise of their marriage. Rita has to study in quiet moments at work and, at one point in the play, we learn that in a fit of temper after finding that Rita is still taking contraceptives, Denny actually burns some of her books.

Rita's mother is an interesting character in as much as, like Rita, she perceives that there is more to life than is being offered to them at present. When she is crying in the pub, she says it is 'because we could sing better songs than those' (p. 46). Rita uses this **metaphor** to stiffen her resolve and work even harder at her education – for it seems the only way out.

Rita, herself, has a vision of the working class which is not entirely favourable. She is dismissive of the working-class culture and states that people are 'either pissed or on the Valium' (p. 30), simply trying to get by. This is what Rita is trying to avoid.

Throughout the play, it is clearly Frank who plays the largest role in 'educating' Rita. However, as the play develops, Rita begins to have other influences in her life. New tutors at summer school introduce her to some of the great poets and Trish, Rita's flatmate, provides a different sort of role model. Once she has overcome her feelings of inferiority towards the other students, Rita is introduced to a whole new peer group. She is no longer afraid to mix with them on the lawns, and her job in the bistro offers even wider social access to their circles.

In the second half of the play, Rita changes quite dramatically as a character. She becomes more confident and takes control of situations herself. Her language changes and she learns to express herself effectively. Her dress sense also undergoes a change as she tries to find her true identity. The change of name from Rita back to Susan is also important in this search. It would be fair to say that, to some extent, Rita does lose herself in this section of the play. The way she changes her voice on the suggestion of Trish is one clear example of a woman who is searching for an identity. However, by the end of the play, Rita has emerged as a confident, articulate character who is perfectly at ease with herself.

FRANK

In the opening scenes the audience receive a rather negative picture of Frank. His drinking is clearly becoming a problem and the reasons for this escapism are deeply ingrained. He is dissatisfied with his role in life. A previous marriage has failed and we soon learn that his present relationship is far from ideal. He is disrespectful towards his students and resents having to use valuable drinking time in the pub on mature students like Rita who have signed up for the Open University course. However, it is his recent inability to write poetry which creates most frustration in Frank.

Rita gives Frank a new lease of life. The windows in his room are stuck fast, and even the door seems reluctant to allow free access. Frank welcomes the way Rita seems to shake him out of his lethargy. Later in the play she tells him that a room is like a plant and that he should open the windows, sensing perhaps that Frank needs change. Rita's personality is refreshing because she is so different from the other students. Her language, although frequently inappropriate for academic circles, is colourful and, by contrast, Frank appears rather dull and lifeless: 'Tragedy in dramatic terms is inevitable, pre-ordained.' (p. 41) The impression the reader receives is that Frank has said this line too many times for it to mean anything to him. Just like Rita, he needs to rediscover himself.

Ironically, the more Rita develops, the less she needs Frank and so his self-esteem deteriorates. He eventually descends into shameful drunkenness, falling off the stage in the middle of his lecture. For

CHECKPOINT 39

What does the summer school provide for Rita?

Tired
Frustrated
In need of change

Frank, witnessing Rita's development is not always a pleasurable experience. He is uneasy about her metamorphosis and is particularly concerned that, for Rita to be successful in her studies, she may have to abandon what he describes as her 'uniqueness'.

Despite the rift with Rita, the ending re-establishes the bond between the two characters. Frank tries to contact Rita about the examination, which demonstrates a genuine care and concern. Furthermore, the present of the dress serves to underline the tenderness and affection with which Frank regards Rita.

MINOR CHARACTERS

Although Frank and Rita are the only two figures to appear on stage, we are introduced to a number of other characters through their words. These minor characters have a significant part to play in the shaping of events in *Educating Rita* and their relevance needs to be emphasised.

CHECK THE NET
www.ontalink.com/ literature/willyrussell In particular, focus on the plays in performance.

Denny

Rita's husband fails to support her attempts to educate herself, which he sees as a threat. He wants her to have children and resents the fact that she does not share his desire.

Julia

Frank's partner is one of his ex-students. After the break-up of his marriage, Frank begins to live with Julia, but even from the beginning of the play it appears that their relationship is rather strained.

Rita's mother

Like Rita, she senses that there must be more to life than her present, mundane existence and is saddened by the feeling that she has wasted her opportunities of fulfilment. Unless Rita acts in a positive manner and changes her lifestyle, the audience suspects that this is how she, too, will end up.

Trish

Rita's flatmate. Following the breakdown of Rita's marriage, Trish becomes a type of role model for Rita, who is desperate to change, and Rita almost idolises her new friend. Only at the end of the play does Rita see Trish for what she really is, when her attempted suicide reflects that she, too, has her own problems and weaknesses.

Tiger

Tiger, so-called because of his surname 'Tyson', seems to be a leading figure among the students. He is a potential love interest for Rita, and Frank certainly appears to be jealous of him when he invites Rita to go to France with his group of friends.

LANGUAGE AND STYLE

Willy Russell was clearly aware of the importance of language in society and within education in particular. *Educating Rita* is principally about a character trying to find the words to express herself and, as she becomes more educated, Rita learns to adapt her language to suit her audience. Instead of sounding incongruous and out of place in the study of a university lecturer, Rita's increasing mastery of the language enables her to grow in confidence as a person.

In creating the character of Rita, Willy Russell was reaching out to an audience whose daily language was neither the language of the university nor of the theatre. In this sense, he was trying to write a play which would attract a whole cross-section of society and that would hold as much meaning for the Ritas in the audience as it would for the Franks.

Whilst avoiding the 'lengthy analysis' that Willy Russell would have scorned, it is fruitful to reflect on the type of language that he uses in the play, particularly as much of the play's humour is derived from Rita's style of talking and the contrast in speech between Frank and Rita. Rita's **accent** and **dialect** clearly pitch her in the working class and clash with Frank's middle-class academic

 DID YOU KNOW?

Willy Russell once said: 'I ...don't want to write plays which are resigned, menopausal, despairing and whining'.

language. In the opening scene of the play, Rita's language is evidently out of place. When talking about the picture of a nude religious scene hanging on Frank's wall, Rita asks her tutor whether or not he thinks of it as erotic. On hearing Frank's reply, 'I suppose it is', Rita's reaction is to state, 'There's no suppose about it. Look at those tits' (p. 3).

The mismatch between Rita's coarse and vulgar language and the academic setting of the play is frequently the source of humour in *Educating Rita*, but occasionally Willy Russell uses Rita's lack of knowledge to include verbal jokes at the character's expense. One such example comes when Frank asks Rita a question about poetry. 'Do you know Yeats?' says Frank. 'The wine lodge?' (p. 8) comes the reply. In the second half of the play, however, it is Rita who makes the jokes herself as her newly found confidence, borne from a growing mastery of the language, comes to the fore. She relates how, at the summer school, a tutor asked if she liked Ferlinghetti and comments how the old Rita would have said 'only with Parmesan cheese'. Instead, her reply is a carefully controlled and serious response: 'Actually I'm not too familiar with the American poets' (p. 50).

Similarly, in the first half of the play, the way she talks about the performance of *Macbeth* reflects her enthusiasm and her growing passion for literature without possessing the language to discuss and analyse: 'But listen, it wasn't borin', it was bleedin' great.'. Frank on the other hand, uses carefully measured tones: 'Tragedy in dramatic terms is inevitable, pre-ordained' (p. 41). His vocabulary, however, is rather jaded and lethargic, as though he has made this speech countless times before. The **irony** of this exchange is that, although Rita does not possess the vocabulary to fully articulate her thoughts, the ideas that she does express are clearly on the right lines. Describing Lady Macbeth as 'a cow' (p. 40) and **assonance** as 'gettin' the rhyme wrong' (p. 8), may, at first, seem laughable and inappropriate, but on reflection they are seen to be Rita's early attempts to find a suitable voice to express literary concepts and are refreshing in contrast to a typical academic response. Indeed, it is Rita's vibrant language which helps to enthuse Frank away from his unmotivated position.

DID YOU KNOW?

Lawrence Ferlinghetti was an American Beat poet, who co-founded a publishing house called City Light Books. He was arrested in 1956 for publishing Allen Ginsberg's *Howl*, all about Trotskyites, Junkies and 'Queers'.

LANGUAGE AND STYLE

In the second half of the play, Rita attempts to change her speech when Trish, her flatmate, advises that 'beautiful literature' should not be discussed in an 'ugly voice' (p. 56). However, what Rita fails to realise is that her language is inextricably linked with her personality. Noticeably, at the end of the play when Rita is confident in the knowledge that she has passed the examination, her natural speech returns. Having rejected the false name of Rita in favour of her original name, Susan, she also rejects all the falseness of her affected speech.

In the same way that Rita's language changes, Frank picks up several of her phrases such as 'completely off my cake' (p. 60) and even resorts to swearing in the same style as Rita did at the beginning of the play.

Rita's coarseness, in itself, is humorous because it is so inappropriate: 'God, I've had enough of this. It's borin', that's what it is, bloody borin'. This Forster, honest to God he doesn't half get on my tits' (p. 24). Frank's dry response of 'Good. You must show me the evidence' adds to the humour. This verbal sparring is between two completely different characters, coming from wildly contrasting backgrounds. Culture and language clash head on.

The ending of the play is cleverly controlled by Russell. When Rita tells Frank that there is just one thing left that she can do for him in order to say thank you for his teaching, the audience detects more than a hint of a sexual undertone. The comic ending is achieved when the tension of the final scene is alleviated by Rita taking out a pair of scissors and preparing to cut Frank's hair.

The form that the play takes is that of a 'two-hander', meaning that all the action and dialogue is focused on two central characters. The style of the play is essentially **naturalistic** and, as the only characters to appear on stage are Frank and Rita, other characters such as Denny and Julia, are introduced to the audience through the spoken word. The fact that the whole play is centred in Frank's room at the university also helps to establish the naturalistic feel of *Educating Rita*. By adhering to the **unity** of place, Willy Russell is able to concentrate the audience's attention on the two central

 DID YOU KNOW?

It was very fashionable in the late 1960s for men to grow their hair long, but as this play is set in the mid 1970s, clearly Frank is living a bit in the past.

characters. He is able to highlight Rita's attempts to fit into this alien environment and reflect on the way Frank is prevented from stagnation by the 'breath of air' (p. 11) she brings with her.

CHECK THE BOOK

Pygmalion, by George Bernard Shaw. Compare the characters of Rita and Eliza Doolittle.

In terms of language and identity, another text which has parallels with *Educating Rita* is the play by George Bernard Shaw, *Pygmalion* (also a study guide in this York Notes series). First produced in 1914 and later screened as the film *My Fair Lady*, it tells the story of a poor flower girl called Eliza Doolittle who is taken in by Professor Higgins, an expert in linguistics. He teaches her to speak 'properly' and, just like Rita, she is transformed into an entirely different character. Both plays focus on the development of a central female character but, whereas Professor Higgins concentrates on linguistics with his 'student' Eliza, Frank's main sphere of interest with Rita is English Literature. Both women come from intellectually poor backgrounds and both speak with strong regional accents which hamper their development academically and socially. Of the two, Rita develops as the more rounded character. Eliza's change in language pronunciation is seen as relatively superficial whereas Rita, whose language use does not vary significantly, seems to grow from within. Her language, therefore, is seen as an extension of her character and the two cannot be separated.

PART FOUR

RESOURCES

HOW TO USE QUOTATIONS

One of the secrets of success in writing essays is the way you use quotations. There are five basic principles:

1 Put inverted commas at the beginning and end of the quotation.

2 Write the quotation exactly as it appears in the original.

3 Do not use a quotation that repeats what you have just written.

4 Use the quotation so that it fits into your sentence.

5 Keep the quotation as short as possible.

Quotations should be used to develop the line of thought in your essays. Your comment should not duplicate what is in your quotation. For example:

> **Rita tells Frank that she couldn't go to the dinner party because she had bought the wrong sort of wine 'I couldn't. I'd bought the wrong sort of wine'** (Act I, Scene 7).

Far more effective is to write:

> **Rita explains to Frank that she couldn't go to the dinner party because she had 'bought the wrong sort of wine'** (Act I, Scene 6).

However, the most sophisticated way of using the writer's words is to embed them into your sentence:

> **Rita's emotive appraisal of Macbeth as 'bleedin' great'** (Act I, Scene 6) **reflects a freshness of approach that is entirely lacking in Frank's rather stilted language.**

When you use quotations in this way, you are demonstrating the ability to use text as evidence to support your ideas - not simply including words from the original to prove you have read it.

EXAMINER'S SECRET

In a typical examination you might use as many as eight quotations.

Coursework essay

Set aside an hour or so at the start of your work to plan what you have to do.

- List all the points you feel are needed to cover the task. Collect page references of information and quotations that will support what you have to say. A helpful tool is the highlighter pen: this saves painstaking copying and enables you to target precisely what you want to use.

- Focus on what you consider to be the main points of the essay. Try to sum up your argument in a single sentence, which could be the closing sentence of your essay. Depending on the essay title, it could be a statement about a character: Rita's changing character is reflected in her different ways of speaking, and her partial return to her original accent and dialect suggests a newly acquired confidence within herself; an opinion about a setting: Frank's cluttered office reflects his own feelings of chaos and despair; or a judgement on a theme: I think that, although the title of the play is 'Educating Rita', it is obvious that Frank learns a lot too.

- Make a short essay plan. Use the first paragraph to introduce the argument you wish to make. In the following paragraphs develop this argument with details, examples and other possible points of view. Sum up your argument in the last paragraph. Check you have answered the question.

- Write the essay, remembering all the time the central point you are making.

- On completion, go back over what you have written to eliminate careless errors and improve expression. Read it aloud to yourself, or, if you are feeling more confident, to a relative or friend.

If you can, try to type your essay, using a word processor. This will allow you to correct and improve your writing without spoiling its appearance.

EXAMINER'S SECRET

Examiners **never** take marks away.

SITTING THE EXAMINATION

Examination papers are carefully designed to give you the opportunity to do your best. Follow these handy hints for exam success:

BEFORE YOU START

- Make sure you know the subject of the examination so that you are properly prepared and equipped.

- You need to be comfortable and free from distractions. Inform the invigilator if anything is off-putting, e.g. a shaky desk.

- Read the instructions, or rubric, on the front of the examination paper. You should know by now what you have to do but check to reassure yourself.

- Observe the time allocation – and follow it carefully. If they recommend 60 minutes for Question 1 and 30 minutes for Question 2, it is because Question 1 carries twice as many marks.

- Consider the mark allocation. You should write a longer response for 4 marks than for 2 marks.

WRITING YOUR RESPONSES

- Use the questions to structure your response, e.g. question: 'The endings of X's poems are always particularly significant. Explain their importance with reference to two poems.' The first part of your answer will describe the ending of the first poem; the second part will look at the ending of the second poem; the third part will be an explanation of the significance of the two endings.

- Write a brief draft outline of your response.

- A typical 30-minute examination essay is probably between 400 and 600 words in length.

- Keep your writing legible and easy to read, using paragraphs to show the structure of your answers.

 **EXAMINER'S SECRET**

Always read the whole examination paper before you start writing.

- Spend a couple of minutes afterwards quickly checking for obvious errors.

WHEN YOU HAVE FINISHED

- Don't be downhearted – if you found the examination difficult, it is probably because you really worked at the questions. Let's face it, they are not meant to be easy!

- Don't pay too much attention to what your friends have to say about the paper. Everyone's experience is different and no two people ever give the same answers.

IMPROVE YOUR GRADE

KNOW THE TEXT

Whatever text you are studying, it is vital that you are familiar with its contents. These Notes are intended to help you arrive at a fuller understanding and appreciation of the play, but they are no substitute for reading the text and seeing the play performed on stage.

Essentially, there are three important aspects that you will have to master:

- The development of Rita's character

- The changing relationship of Frank and Rita

- The play in performance

As the central character in the play, your understanding of the character of Rita will ultimately determine the quality of any response that you may be asked for. You need to consider what motivates Rita and to develop a sense of empathy for her character. Use the *Checkpoints* in these Notes to reflect on key issues in more detail. Identify the key moments in the play where Rita's character can be seen to have moved on and make your own notes on these sections.

EXAMINER'S SECRET

Show an awareness that the play has been consciously crafted by the playwright and that choices have been made by the writer to affect the audience's response to characters and events.

Throughout the play, you should be able to chart the changing relationship of Frank and Rita. You could record these changes in note form or, alternatively, try to draw them in the form of a table. Sometimes, making notes in visual or diagrammatic form can make them easier to learn.

Whatever you do, always write about *Educating Rita* as a play that was designed to be performed on stage. Even if you have seen the film version of the play, and it is strongly recommended that you should, you must put this to the back of your mind and imagine the play on stage. An examiner will reward you for your understanding of the craft of a playwright, so be prepared to comment on **how** Russell achieves certain dramatic effects. Clearly, if you have seen the play in performance or tried to stage a scene with some of your friends, you will have a much greater awareness of the key issues.

EXAMINER'S SECRET

Aim to provide an 'overview' so that you show the 'big picture' before moving on to the more specific detailed points.

USING QUOTATIONS

Many of the key quotations are highlighted in the main body of these Notes, but you might also like to keep your own record so that you can find references more quickly. As you note them down, link each quotation with what it illustrates. For instance: 'half-caste' (p. 45) – describes how Rita is trapped between two different worlds.

Remember to use the quotations correctly, indenting longer quotations or working shorter quotations into your own text within quotation marks. It is advised to keep quotations down to a minimum length by selecting the key words and phrases rather than relying on the examiner to extract the necessary information from an overlong quotation for himself.

THEMATIC DEVELOPMENT

Although you obviously need to show an understanding of the characters and what happens in the play, an examiner will also be looking to spot your understanding of the main themes in *Educating Rita*. Read the section on **Themes** in these Notes and keep referring to the text as you seek to *interpret* the play. In particular, focus on these central ideas:

● ENVIRONMENT – Look at how Rita struggles to fit into Frank's world at first and chart her development as she grows in confidence. Focus on how a director would convey this idea on stage through Rita's movement and mannerisms, as well as the more obvious things such as use of costume.

● LANGUAGE – Compare the language used by Frank and Rita and, once again, look closely at how this changes throughout the course of the play.

● EDUCATION – Consider what Frank learns through his association with Rita as well as what education provides for Rita herself and be aware of how each character develops in the play.

BEFORE THE EXAMINATION

Getting your ideas straight

Too often students find themselves with a vast assortment of notes, essays, study guides and videos to plough through … and that's before turning to the play itself! Sometimes it can seem a daunting prospect to start revising from all this material but, if you approach it in the right way, you will surprise yourself with how much you can learn.

The key to successful revision is splitting information up into manageable chunks or segments. For example, aim to condense all your notes on Rita's character on to one sheet of A4 paper, and do the same for Frank. Using bullet points, spider diagrams, charts and other visual forms of note-making can be very useful in helping you to condense a lot of information as well as making it easier to remember.

Once you have a revision sheet for each topic area, the next crucial step is to make sure that you have all the key quotations to support your points. Keep these on a separate sheet but cross-refer them with all your other notes.

THE EXAMINATION

Read the question

Failing to read the question correctly is probably the most frequent reason why students fail to achieve their potential in examinations. Make sure that you read the question that has been set rather than the one you hoped would be set! Identify the key words in the examination question and underline them before planning your response.

Always answer each part of a question. For example, look closely at the following question: **'As the director of *Educating Rita*, what ideas would you want to put across to the audience and how would you ensure that you were successful?'** This is quite a complex question to answer. Here, you are required to imagine that you are a director of the play and then you have to answer a question that is in two parts:

- What ideas do you want to put across to the audience?

- How would you ensure that these ideas were conveyed successfully?

Most students would be able to make a reasonable attempt at the first part of the question because it deals with things such as characters and relationships. It is much more difficult, however, to make a successful response to the second part of the question. This deals with the notion of stagecraft, so it is here that you would be expected to draw on your knowledge and understanding of dramatic devices, structures and techniques.

To avoid the second part of the question would limit your response significantly and it is likely that an examiner would only credit you with a basic level of achievement.

 **EXAMINER'S SECRET**
Keep the question visible at all times during the writing of your answer and keep referring to it so that you continue to stay 'on track'.

EXAM TECHNIQUE

There are many tips that you can learn that will help you succeed in examinations, so listen carefully to the advice that is given by teachers, tutors, parents or even friends who have already been through the process of sitting formal exams. As you will see from the *Examiner's Secrets* in these Notes, there are some fairly basic things that you need to address if you want to succeed, but the main two are:

EXAMINER'S SECRET

Always use appropriate quotations both to illustrate points and to extend your argument. Never leave quotations 'hanging' with no specific function.

- STRUCTURE – make sure that you answer the question directly and frame your response in this way:

  Introduction: This should be a brief paragraph that outlines your response to the question and shows the examiner that you have a clear 'overview' of the question.

  Main body: Following your **general** introduction, the main body of your essay should focus on **specific** points. Deal with each one in a separate paragraph and remember to provide lots of detailed textual references to illustrate your points. Remember PQD….Point, Quotation, Development, and you won't go far wrong!

  Conclusion: This should summarise your response and leave the examiner with a favourable impression of your ability to see the 'big picture'. Avoid lengthy paragraphs that repeat points you have made earlier in the essay in favour of a shorter, more pertinent paragraph that rounds off the response effectively.

- TIMING – Don't rush into an answer…always spend an appropriate amount of time thinking and planning your response. A few minutes thinking through an answer at the start may save a lot of time later in the examination.

  As you are writing your answer, keep an eye on the clock and check that you are still sticking to the task! Don't let your concentration wander – make sure that all your points are relevant to the question that has been set.

  Always follow advice given on the examination paper itself. If you are advised to answer two questions, spending one hour on each, then stick to this. Even if you know one of your texts a lot better than another, the few extra marks gained by spending more time on this text will not compensate for those marks lost by writing only a brief answer to your second text.

What the examiners are looking for

Basically, examiners are looking for evidence of your understanding of the characters, plot and themes of *Educating Rita*, as well as an appreciation of the play in performance. However, after a course of study, most students will have been able to arrive a fairly clear grasp of the play, so what will distinguish an average student from one aiming to achieve a higher grade?

Let's consider the possible treatment of the following question: 'As the director of *Educating Rita*, what ideas would you want to put across to the audience and how would you ensure that you were successful?'

Average grade

An average student will focus on the question and write a response that deals directly with the text, as in this extract:

> I would want the audience to see how Rita changes in the play. She starts off uneducated but at the end of the play she is educated. This gives her the chance to choose what she will do with the rest of her life: 'I dunno. I might go to France. I might go to me mother's. I might even have a baby. I dunno. I'll make a decision. I'll choose' (pp. 72–3).

> Another thing I would want the audience to realise is how Frank's drinking gets worse throughout the play.

The student uses an appropriate quotation but fails to put the quotation into its proper context and does not expand the point. Simple, direct statements will be rewarded by the examiner, but to achieve the higher grades you will be expected to extend ideas and sustain a point of view. Look again how the student makes the point about Rita's ability to choose what she will do before rushing on to the next point about Frank. This lack of development will limit the marks that an examiner can award this student.

Also, note how the student focuses specifically on the ideas s/he wants to put across to the audience without considering how s/he is

EXAMINER'S SECRET

Remember to discuss *Educating Rita* as a piece of stagecraft as opposed to simply being words on a page.

EXAMINER'S SECRET

Spend time reading, thinking and planning before answering any questions. Make sure you choose the right question for you rather than rushing blindly into an answer.

going to do this. In this sense, the student is only answering half the question that has been set.

Higher grade

The following extract is a more developed, considered response that would earn one of the higher grades in an examination:

> As a director of the play, one of the main points that I would want to convey to the audience is how Rita's education has transformed her life. Visually, this could be done through the use of appropriate costumes, with Rita's clothes in the final scene representing how she has become a 'new woman'. Although this transformation has been painful, resulting in Rita's broken marriage, it does leave Rita with a sense of liberation. For example, when Frank asks her what she intends to do, she replies, 'I dunno. I might go to France. I might go to me mother's. I might even have a baby. I dunno. I'll make a decision. I'll choose' (pp. 72–3). It is this ability to choose her own destiny that makes her so different from the Rita at the start of the play and I would emphasise this transformation by....

Notice how the student is sustaining a response and focusing in more detail on **how** the ideas could be conveyed to the audience. This is clearly going to be a full response that covers all aspects of the question and deals directly with the text in some detail. The student uses the same quotation as in the previous extract, but places it in context and uses it to develop the point further. Also, note the sophisticated use of vocabulary that is the hallmark of a higher-grade candidate.

Now take a break!

SAMPLE ESSAY PLAN

A typical essay question on *Educating Rita* is followed by a sample essay plan in note form. This does not represent the only answer to the question, merely one answer. Do not be afraid to include your own ideas, and leave out some of those in the sample. Remember that quotations are seential to prove and illustrate the points you make.

Examine Frank's growing sense of unease as Rita becomes more educated.

Such a question anticipates a carefully focused response.

PART 1: INTRODUCTION

Establish that, in the early scenes, it is Frank who is in control. Look at his use of language and compare it to the way Rita speaks, showing how this partly prevents her from being fully accepted in Frank's world.

PART 2: RITA'S GROWING CONFIDENCE

Look closely at Rita's change in character in Act II, Scene 1, after attending the summer school. She tells Frank that she has already

EXAMINER'S SECRET
Wide reading will shine through! Although an examination essay will need to focus on this play in particular, reading other plays and works by the same author will enable you to put ideas in context and make meaningful comparisons where appropriate.

'done' Blake (p. 56). Other lecturers besides Frank have begun to have a bearing on her development. Rita also mentions Trish, who has become another influence in her life. Give examples.

PART 3: FRANK'S JEALOUSY

Look at Frank's reaction when Rita is invited to go to France with Tiger and his friends. Are the reasons he gives for her not going simply excuses? Consider the way he treats Rita when she tries to change her way of speaking (Act II, Scene 2). He implores, 'Rita! Just be yourself' (p. 57). Is he failing to understand that Rita does not want to be 'herself', and that she is trying to escape her situation by becoming educated?

EXAMINER'S SECRET

An A-grade candidate can analyse a variety of the writer's techniques.

PART 4: RITA'S 'UNIQUENESS' DISAPPEARS

Consider the way Frank becomes appalled at what he has created in Rita. Why does he liken himself to Mary Shelley who wrote the novel *Frankenstein*? He feels that she has changed, and not for the better, saying that when she writes, 'there's nothing of you in there' (p. 62). When she is late for a tutorial, he asks, 'perhaps you don't want to waste your time coming here anymore?' (p. 65). Is this a sign of Frank's own insecurity?

PART 5: CONCLUSION

Reflect on the final scene and how both characters seem to have come to terms with themselves and appear to be more settled, despite the fact that neither of them is sure what the future holds. Think about Frank's present of the dress. Does this symbolise his acceptance that Rita has matured into an educated woman?

FURTHER QUESTIONS

❶ What does Rita gain from her 'education' and what does she lose?

❷ Compare and contrast the way Rita and Frank use language throughout *Educating Rita*.

❸ Rita describes herself as a 'half-caste' (Act I, Scene 7), neither fitting comfortably into her own society or that of Frank. How appropriate would it be to describe Frank in that way?

❹ Look closely at Act I, Scenes 6–7. Explain why Frank invites Rita to dinner and, ultimately, why she fails to turn up.

❺ Explore Willy Russell's use of humour in the play.

❻ Although *Educating Rita* is a comedy, Willy Russell develops a number of serious issues in the play. Select those issues which you feel are most important and examine his treatment of them in detail.

❼ This play is about educating Rita. Frank also learns a lot about himself, but what have you learned from the play?

❽ Is the play still as relevant today as it was when it was first written?

❾ Select the three scenes in the play which you find most dramatic and explain why they are so powerful.

❿ As the director of the play, what ideas would you want to put across to the audience and how would you ensure that you were successful?

CHECK THE FILM

Educating Rita (1983), directed by Lewis Gilbert, stars Julie Walters and Michael Caine. Look at the additional scenes required to translate the play meaningfully from stage to screen.

analogy suggestion of a likeness between two things

antithesis opposing or contrasting ideas

assonance the repetition of vowel sounds

dialect accent and vocabulary which vary due to social and regional background

irony saying one thing while you mean another, often through understatement, concealment or indirect statement

metaphor an image where something is described as being something else, not to be read literally

naturalistic in drama, referring to the staging of a play which is essentially realistic

parody a deliberately exaggerated imitation

playwright the writer of a play

plot the storyline or main narrative thread

setting the place where the action on stage is set

stage directions advice printed in the text of a play giving instructions or information about the movements, gestures and appearance of the actors, or on the special effects required at a particular moment in the action

structure the way a work of literature has been pieced together, a framework

symbolism the practice of using symbols to represent something else

theme a repeated idea which has a prominent place in the play

tragedy a serious play which ends in misfortune

unity relating to the classical unities which governed the structure of plays, for example the unity of place which proposed that stage action should be limited to one set in order to make the play more realistic

CHECKPOINT 1 Willy Russell and Rita were born and raised in Liverpool. Both failed with their education first time round but made a successful return to learning as adults. Both worked as ladies' hairdressers.

CHECKPOINT 2 Denny is desperate for Rita to have a baby that will limit her ability to change in the future. He chooses to go to the pub rather than Frank's dinner party, and he burns all Rita's books when he finds out she is still taking the contraceptive pill.

CHECKPOINT 3 The way Rita struggles with the door knob and then clumsily falls through the door makes the audience aware that she does not fit in very well with this environment. Her clothes would set her apart from the 'proper students' and her language would make her seem out of place.

CHECKPOINT 4 Lots! Look for examples of Rita's use of colloquial language or swearing and contrast these with examples of Frank's heightened vocabulary or academic jargon.

CHECKPOINT 5 Who knows? There is the possibility that Denny and Rita could have changed and grown together rather than growing apart, but it does seem as though the two characters want different things from their lives.

CHECKPOINT 6 Frank's jealousy drives a wedge between them.

CHECKPOINT 7 Look at Act 1, Scene 2.

CHECKPOINT 8 The main source of humour comes from the language in the play; there is a great contrast between Frank's and Rita's use of language. Rita's language often sounds incongruous and out of place and her inappropriate language is often a source of comedy.

CHECKPOINT 9 Rita feels out of place herself, drawing a distinction between herself and the 'proper' students. Her lack of knowledge and understanding from her previous education has resulted in low self-esteem. Her clothes and her use of language also set her apart and make her feel out of place.

CHECKPOINT 10 Rita is so forceful that he doesn't have much choice! There is evidence to suggest that he is attracted to her and he also finds her interesting because she is so different to all his other students.

CHECKPOINT 11 The main problem facing Rita is trying to balance work and studying. This is made more difficult because of Denny's lack of support. Although Rita lacks confidence, she makes up for this with her determination.

CHECKPOINT 12 Frank says 'Rita, why didn't you walk in here twenty years ago?' Look for other examples of his flirting. He clearly enjoys her company and invites her to the dinner party.

CHECKPOINT 13 Rita begins to adapt her language and to understand the books she is studying, even going to the theatre to see *Macbeth*. Frank begins to learn about himself: why he is unable to write poetry any more and, possibly, why he drinks so much.

CHECKPOINT 14 See Checkpoint 5. It would appear that their marriage was destined to fail with Rita unable to tell Denny the truth about staying on the pill and Denny's lack of support for Rita's return to education, culminating in the burning of her books.

CHECKPOINT 15 Rita feels as though there is no such thing. All she sees is 'everyone pissed, or on the Valium, tryin' to get from one day to the next' (p. 30).

CHECKPOINT 16 Rita's *Peer Gynt* essay is the first time that we see signs of her ability to use the type of academic language that will see her through the exams.

CHECKPOINT 17 Frank drinks possibly because of his frustrations at not being able to write the kind of poetry he would like. Also, there is evidence to suggest that he loathes his job, and his history of failed relationships adds to his problems.

CHECKPOINT 18 Frank has genuine affection for Rita and enjoys her company. He finds her interesting because she is so different from all the other students. Possibly, he sees the dinner party as part of her wider education.

CHECKPOINT 19 Rita's lack of confidence prevents her from going to the dinner party. She feels out of place and fears that people will laugh at her for wearing the wrong clothes or taking the wrong sort of wine.

CHECKPOINT 20 Rita describes herself as a 'half-caste' because she feels trapped between two worlds. She no longer feels comfortable in her life as a hairdresser and yet she knows that she doesn't fit easily into the role of a university student either.

CHECKPOINT 21 In the pub, Rita sees her mum crying which seems to reflect a deep sadness. Not wanting to end up the same way, Rita uses this to spur her on with her education.

CHECKPOINT 22 Rita uses the break-up of her marriage to work even harder with her studies.

CHECKPOINT 23 At the start of Act II, Rita's entrance is very different from the start of the play. She is more assured and confident.

CHECKPOINT 24 After the interval, Rita appears more confident and less in need of Frank's influence.

CHECKPOINT 25 The audience starts to feel sympathy for Frank. Before the interval, despite his drink problem, Frank was perceived as the stronger character of the two. Now that Rita no longer needs him in quite the same way, we become more aware of his own frailty.

CHECKPOINT 26 Sitting with the others down on the grass means that Rita finally feels like a 'proper' student.

CHECKPOINT 27 Frank's jealousy starts to take hold and he behaves irrationally.

CHECKPOINT 28 The opening of Act II, Scene 3 is unusual because the lights come up on Rita rather than Frank, underlining the fact that Rita is now seen as the one who is more 'in control'.

CHECKPOINT 29 Frank is critical of Rita's work because it seems to lack passion and feeling. He feels that she has lost her 'uniqueness' (p. 48).

CHECKPOINT 30 Frank gives Rita the poems as a kind of test to see if she will respond openly and honestly.

CHECKPOINT 31 Rita reverts to her original name of Susan because, as she says, calling herself by a different name was 'pretentious crap' (p. 69). She was trying to be someone else but now accepts that she has found her true self.

CHECKPOINT 32 Despite all their arguments, Frank has genuine affection for Rita. He realises that she has progressed so far that it is right for Rita to complete her education by sitting the examination.

CHECKPOINT 33 Frank is packing all his belongings into crates bound for Australia, having been sent away by the university authorities.

CHECKPOINT 34 Education gives Rita the power to choose what she will do with the rest of her life but it comes at the expense of her marriage, and she also loses her job and her home.

CHECKPOINT 35 The cutting of Frank's hair is symbolic. His long hair is representative of a bygone era and Frank is seemingly trapped in the past. Going to Australia is seen as a new start for Frank.

CHECKPOINT 36 There seems little hope for Frank who is slowly drinking himself to an early grave. Australia represents his best bet for a new and better life where, hopefully, he will find fulfilment both as a writer and in his personal relationships, and give him the impetus to curb his drinking.

CHECKPOINT 37 Rita makes the mistake of being 'dazzled' by people such as Trish and Tiger, almost hero-worshipping them. By the end of the play, she sees them for who they really are.

CHECKPOINT 38 Frank talks about his own 'appalling teaching' and feels that it is 'quite in order for most of my appalling students' (p. 13), but he is clearly very different with Rita. He recognises that Rita is not like all the other students and that he can make a difference so he is enthused by the prospect of educating Rita.

CHECKPOINT 39 Summer school introduces Rita to new poets, gives her the chance to make new friends and meet new tutors other than Frank. Above all though, it provides her with the opportunity to grow in confidence.

TEST ANSWERS

TEST YOURSELF (ACT I, SCENES 1–4)

1 Rita

2 Frank

3 Rita

4 Rita

5 Roger McGough

6 Rita Mae Brown

7 E.M. Forster

8 Henrik Ibsen

TEST YOURSELF (ACT I, SCENES 5–8)

1 Rita

2 Frank

3 Denny

4 Julia

5 Macbeth

6 Rita's mother

TEST YOURSELF (ACT II, SCENES 1–3)

1 Trish (through Rita)

2 Rita

3 Rita

4 Rita

5 Trish

6 Tiger

7 The university authorities

8 Frank's regular students

TEST YOURSELF (ACT II, SCENES 4–7)

1 Frank

2 Rita

3 Frank

4 Rita

5 The students Rita meets at the bistro

6 Trish

7 Rita

Maya Angelou
I Know Why the Caged Bird Sings

Jane Austen
Pride and Prejudice

Alan Ayckbourn
Absent Friends

Elizabeth Barrett Browning
Selected Poems

Robert Bolt
A Man for All Seasons

Harold Brighouse
Hobson's Choice

Charlotte Brontë
Jane Eyre

Emily Brontë
Wuthering Heights

Shelagh Delaney
A Taste of Honey

Charles Dickens
David Copperfield
Great Expectations
Hard Times
Oliver Twist

Roddy Doyle
Paddy Clarke Ha Ha Ha

George Eliot
Silas Marner
The Mill on the Floss

Anne Frank
The Diary of a Young Girl

William Golding
Lord of the Flies

Oliver Goldsmith
She Stoops to Conquer

Willis Hall
The Long and the Short and the Tall

Thomas Hardy
Far from the Madding Crowd

The Mayor of Casterbridge
Tess of the d'Urbervilles
The Withered Arm and other Wessex Tales

L.P. Hartley
The Go-Between

Seamus Heaney
Selected Poems

Susan Hill
I'm the King of the Castle

Barry Hines
A Kestrel for a Knave

Louise Lawrence
Children of the Dust

Harper Lee
To Kill a Mockingbird

Laurie Lee
Cider with Rosie

Arthur Miller
The Crucible
A View from the Bridge

Robert O'Brien
Z for Zachariah

Frank O'Connor
My Oedipus Complex and Other Stories

George Orwell
Animal Farm

J.B. Priestley
An Inspector Calls
When We Are Married

Willy Russell
Educating Rita
Our Day Out

J.D. Salinger
The Catcher in the Rye

William Shakespeare
Henry IV Part I
Henry V
Julius Caesar

Macbeth
The Merchant of Venice
A Midsummer Night's Dream
Much Ado About Nothing
Romeo and Juliet
The Tempest
Twelfth Night

George Bernard Shaw
Pygmalion

Mary Shelley
Frankenstein

R.C. Sherriff
Journey's End

Rukshana Smith
Salt on the snow

John Steinbeck
Of Mice and Men

Robert Louis Stevenson
Dr Jekyll and Mr Hyde

Jonathan Swift
Gulliver's Travels

Robert Swindells
Daz 4 Zoe

Mildred D. Taylor
Roll of Thunder, Hear My Cry

Mark Twain
Huckleberry Finn

James Watson
Talking in Whispers

Edith Wharton
Ethan Frome

William Wordsworth
Selected Poems

A Choice of Poets

Mystery Stories of the Nineteenth Century including The Signalman

Nineteenth Century Short Stories

Poetry of the First World War

Six Women Poets

Margaret Atwood
Cat's Eye
The Handmaid's Tale

Jane Austen
Emma
Mansfield Park
Persuasion
Pride and Prejudice
Sense and Sensibility

Alan Bennett
Talking Heads

William Blake
Songs of Innocence and of Experience

Charlotte Brontë
Jane Eyre
Villette

Emily Brontë
Wuthering Heights

Angela Carter
Nights at the Circus

Geoffrey Chaucer
The Franklin's Prologue and Tale
The Miller's Prologue and Tale
The Prologue to the Canterbury Tales
The Wife of Bath's Prologue and Tale

Samuel Coleridge
Selected Poems

Joseph Conrad
Heart of Darkness

Daniel Defoe
Moll Flanders

Charles Dickens
Bleak House
Great Expectations
Hard Times

Emily Dickinson
Selected Poems

John Donne
Selected Poems

Carol Ann Duffy
Selected Poems

George Eliot
Middlemarch
The Mill on the Floss

T.S. Eliot
Selected Poems
The Waste Land

F. Scott Fitzgerald
The Great Gatsby

E.M. Forster
A Passage to India

Brian Friel
Translations

Thomas Hardy
Jude the Obscure
The Mayor of Casterbridge
The Return of the Native
Selected Poems
Tess of the d'Urbervilles

Seamus Heaney
Selected Poems from 'Opened Ground'

Nathaniel Hawthorne
The Scarlet Letter

Homer
The Iliad
The Odyssey

Aldous Huxley
Brave New World

Kazuo Ishiguro
The Remains of the Day

Ben Jonson
The Alchemist

James Joyce
Dubliners

John Keats
Selected Poems

Christopher Marlowe
Doctor Faustus
Edward II

Arthur Miller
Death of a Salesman

John Milton
Paradise Lost Books I & II

Toni Morrison
Beloved

George Orwell
Nineteen Eighty-Four

Sylvia Plath
Selected Poems

Alexander Pope
Rape of the Lock & Selected Poems

William Shakespeare
Antony and Cleopatra
As You Like It
Hamlet
Henry IV Part I
King Lear
Macbeth
Measure for Measure
The Merchant of Venice
A Midsummer Night's Dream
Much Ado About Nothing
Othello
Richard II
Richard III
Romeo and Juliet
The Taming of the Shrew
The Tempest
Twelfth Night
The Winter's Tale

George Bernard Shaw
Saint Joan

Mary Shelley
Frankenstein

Jonathan Swift
Gulliver's Travels and A Modest Proposal

Alfred Tennyson
Selected Poems

Virgil
The Aeneid

Alice Walker
The Color Purple

Oscar Wilde
The Importance of Being Earnest

Tennessee Williams
A Streetcar Named Desire

Jeanette Winterson
Oranges Are Not the Only Fruit

John Webster
The Duchess of Malfi

Virginia Woolf
To the Lighthouse

W.B. Yeats
Selected Poems

Metaphysical Poets

THE ULTIMATE WEB SITE FOR THE ULTIMATE LITERATURE GUIDES

At York Notes we believe in helping you achieve exam success. Log on to **www.yorknotes.com** and see how we have made revision even easier, with over 300 titles available to download twenty-four hours a day. The downloads have lots of additional features such as pop-up boxes providing instant glossary definitions, user-friendly links to every part of the guide, and scanned illustrations offering visual appeal. All you need to do is log on to **www.yorknotes.com** and download the books you need to help you achieve exam success.

KEY FEATURES:

Details on how York Notes can help you

Menu Bar to help you find your way around the site

Details on how to download York Notes

Quick Search facility to help you find the titles you need

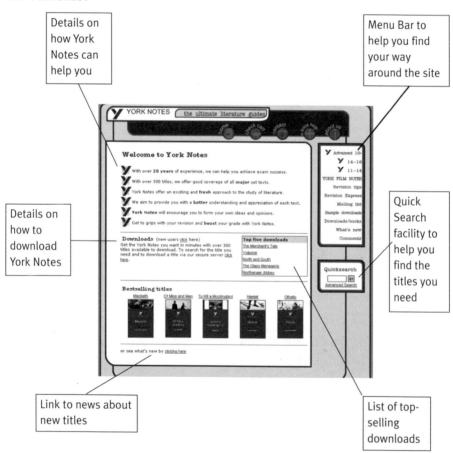

Link to news about new titles

List of top-selling downloads